Insights into
THE UNSEEN
WORLD

IAN ARCHER

WESTBOW
PRESS®
A DIVISION OF THOMAS NELSON
& ZONDERVAN

WestBow Press books may be ordered through booksellers or by contacting:

WestBow Press
A Division of Thomas Nelson & Zondervan
1663 Liberty Drive
Bloomington, IN 47403
www.westbowpress.com
844-714-3454

ISBN: 979-8-3850-1538-2 (sc)
ISBN: 979-8-3850-1539-9 (e)

Library of Congress Control Number: 2023924376

Print information available on the last page.

WestBow Press rev. date: 01/18/2024

CONTENTS

PREFACE

The entire history of man has been marked by discovery; the realization that concepts and other realities exist outside of the scope of what we may know and hold to be true at a specific point in time.

We know much about the natural world and many would concede that there is much more that is to be learned, but what do we know about the unseen world around us? Does it exist and if it does, why? Is there more that we can learn and how can we get that knowledge?

There are three basic groups of individuals on the earth: those who believe in a supreme being(s), (the God of the bible or other gods); those who do not (atheists) and those who say that they are not sure (agnostics). There are many different explanations put forth by persons for why they hold the beliefs that place them in one of the aforementioned categories. All of their views are usually subjective, in spite of the force of the argument, the strength of the logic or the depth of the wit involved.

In this writing, a biblical perspective will be advanced, with the hope of helping those who find themselves in any of the three groups outlined above, to gain a better understanding of the our existence in this realm, in light of *biblical* insights.

In many cultures, there is an established acceptance of the reality of the spiritual nature of man. Few would disagree that man is composed of tangible and intangible parts; a physical body with soul (mind, will, & emotions) and spirit. In western civilization, the body has been extensively studied and dissected for many years, marginal inroads have been made into studies of the mind, but little is known about man's spiritual nature. However, these spiritual realities are quite popular in and infuse the cultures of native North & South American, African and Asian peoples. Their knowledge and understanding of various energies, also called 'chi', prana etc., and the interaction of these energies on and in humans are well known. The recorded histories of these peoples document their attempt to explain the spiritual aspect of our existence, but without knowledge of the One, True God; the God of the Bible. The bible does not hesitate to speak plainly about the reality of a spirit realm. It gives insights into that which we cannot see and this esoteric writing, is a brief study into some of what the bible reveals about the world unseen.

The bible, in my opinion, offers answers to life's most perplexing questions and is used as a reference for truth in this study because of the foundational belief that God is all knowing. He is the only being with a 360 degree perspective on any issue, making what He says absolutely true, whether we agree or not. Fallible men however, have extremely limited perspectives because of our limited grasp on reality, so that we can only have partial truths on many matters.

The bible is composed of individual books, written by multiple men, over the course of many centuries, as they were *inspired* by God. The writings have consistent themes that revolve around the sovereignty of God, the fallen state of man and the various means God used to restore the broken relationship He has with man. It is not just another collection of religious writings, nor are its writings mythical. It gives insights into the past, speaks to us of the present and boldly tells of what the future holds. There is no other book like the bible in the entire world. It does not attempt or claim to answer *every* question we may have, but it does answer every question we need to make it through life. Whether or not we accept its offerings is simply a matter of choice!

I hope that this work is of some benefit to the reader.

CHAPTER ONE

... And There was War

Through faith we understand that the worlds were framed by the word of God, so that things which are seen were not made of things which do appear (Heb. 11:3 KJV)

And there was war in heaven: Michael and his angels fought against the dragon; and the dragon fought and his angels, and prevailed not; neither was their place found any more in heaven. And the great dragon was cast out, that old serpent, called the Devil and Satan, which deceiveth the whole world: he was cast out into the earth and his angels were cast out with him (Rev. 12:7-9 KJV)

The true nature of man (male and female humans) and the world around him (them) cannot be seen solely with the natural senses. We should not be surprised then, that the world that we see around us with all of its wonders to behold, the sights, sounds and conundrums that appear, were made of things that are unseen. They did not evolve or come about through a series of statistically impossible accidents. The bible teaches that the existence of the world and all of its contents was the deliberate act of an unseen, omnipotent, but knowable God.

The two passages above serve to further advance our understanding of the biblical perspective regarding our world and our existence. They highlight several things that are essential to understanding the theme of this book.

Firstly, the passages above state there are both visible and invisible realms, both of which were created. In the physical world, things that are seen are made of things that are tangible; made of matter. However, the things from which matter is made, did not initially exist, they came about, by God's creative power, from things that were not seen.[1] So God made the atoms, and molecules that would form the basis of matter, and the forces that hold them together from nothing.

To draw a parallel, consider that the bible teaches that man is made in the image of God and as such also has creative power.[2] If we consider the processes that precede the natural creation of things by man, we must realize that it starts off in the unseen realm of the mind, so that something unseen in the mind can result in the manifestation of something seen by the eye. The mind can conceive of a thing, and then use the hands to fashion that thing to physically represent the idea. We use trees to make wood, we use that wood to make houses, furniture and a myriad of other items. We extract iron ore from the earth and process it to make steel, which can then be used to make other objects, but

---

[1]   Col. 1:16-20 KJV
[2]   Gen. 1:27 KJV

at the very beginning was the invisible idea. The bible expressly states that this is the same principle that God used when He created the world. He had an idea for the universe and the world; the various species of birds, fish, and plants etc., and by the power of His word, was able to speak it into being; He was able to create that which is seen from nothing.

Secondly, it tells us that it takes faith to understand how God made them. We are familiar with the phrase "seeing is believing"; this is a statement that typifies faithlessness. In the spiritual realm and based on God's creative process, *believing precedes seeing*. This is why in order to see or understand the unseen things of God, one must first use faith.

Faith is the ability to be 'persuaded', to believe something.[3] Since man was created to have a relationship with God, he has the *ability* to believe what God, who only speaks truth, said about a thing without seeing it first. This ability He gave man called faith[4], allows him to conceive and believe in something unseen, so that man could 'create' like God did. The principle then is that what a person believes becomes real or true *to them*. Unfortunately, this ability was not lost after the fall and a person can believe a lie or the truth with equal ferocity and then enact a plan for it to manifest.

Consider that for many years, there have been various incarnations of a teaching some readers may be familiar with called the 'law of attraction'. The basic premise is that 'like attracts like' and by using your thoughts (mental imagery) you can create

---

[3]   Strongs 4102
[4]   Rom 12:3

— 3 —

a desired reality. Millions have invested in books written by a number of authors, who have made these assertions and many actors, athletes, talk show hosts and others have testified of having achieved success which they attributed to following those principles.

On the basis of the faith principle outlined above, we are now able to understand how this happens. The question I would ask is why is it so difficult to believe that if there is a God and if He is more intelligent and powerful than humans, that He is also able to create by the power of his thoughts and words? If ones creations are proportional to their faith and power, then couldn't He create far more fascinating things than we could imagine if His faith and power are unlimited?

It is this that brings us to the third point.

The second passage of scripture above tells us that there is a devil, that he is in the earth and that he deceives the *whole* earth. From the very outset these statements are at variance with the scientific mind and the pervasive humanist philosophies that exist in the Western world, for despite the prevalence of evil in the world and the ubiquitous struggle between good and evil, many do not believe in the existence of a 'devil'. The bible, however, assures us that he is real.

We are further informed that in heaven, before the creation of man, there was a war in heaven as a high ranking angel, who was to become the devil, and a group of angels desired to overthrow God and establish their own dominion. Perfection was forever marred, as an angel entertained the idea that he could become more, have more and do more than was apportioned to him by his Creator. Is this not a manifestation of the faith principle described above and is this not the very root of the concept of sin; the elevating one's own will and desire above God's?

It is here that we first see the emergence of the concept of 'self interest'; an individualism that detaches itself from and seeks to elevates itself above God, in order to cater to its own interests. It is at the heart of all evil that manifests in creation.

The devil not only contrived a plan in his heart, but recruited other angels who were also seduced by the idea of *more* and launched an attempt to displace the Almighty, All knowing God. This attempted coup was averted by beings with less power than God Himself, the archangel Michael and angels in support of God, teaching us several things.

Firstly, despite their great intelligence and knowledge, angels have the ability to make decisions that have consequences beyond their powers of comprehension. Secondly, there are other created beings, lesser in power than God, but more powerful than satan is. So in heaven, there are ranks of power and authority. God Himself did not even bother to get directly involved in this matter, as there was no real threat to His sovereignty. As a consequence of their sin, the devil and his angels, they were banished from eternity into the realm of time and matter, to await God's final judgment. Thirdly, that banishment simply moved the resistance against God from eternity into this more temporal realm.

When God created man, He gave him the authority to be the territorial ruler over earth and *all* in it, including the devil and his angels.[5] Therefore note that, the earth is the domain of

---

[5]   Gen. 1: 28, Job 1:7

man, **not** of God and that is why God works *with* and *through* man to accomplish His will in the earth. He does not force or impose His will in the earth. It was and is God's intent that man would be His representative through whom He would exercise His authority in the earth.

Recalling the 'faith principle,' we know that whatever a person can imagine, good or evil, they can create, *if they believe it*, since they are made in the image of God. The key then is for the devil to persuade men of the things **he** wants them to believe. For ideas are the seed of action, and actions can change, create or cause to manifest, new belief systems, cultures, religions or laws in a society. It is this creative ability that makes man so useful to the devil. For, the devil could accomplish nothing in the earth if not for hijacking and perverting mans God given ability to create what he believes, by faith. So, while banished on earth, the devil has continued his war against God, usurping mans authority to rule and working *through* man, using him as a pawn in his struggle against God. The primary way he did this is by seducing man with the same 'self-interest' that caused his fall. The passage above also allows us to see that the devil has had immense success, as it states that he has deceived the *whole* world. If this assertion is true, then it has immense implications for how the belief systems and cultures found in the world came into being. These belief systems are inclusive of but not limited to concepts of right and wrong, politics, economics, music and arts, religion, the very notion of love, family and even the reality of God Himself. We will explore these thoughts in further detail later on.

Please note that it is not so much that God is at war with satan, since he is no match for Him, as it is that satan continues to oppose God's plans and purposes in the earth until his time in this realm, runs out.

It is in this way that the war that started in heaven continues in earth.

CHAPTER TWO

We Are Spirits

... God, the Father of spirits.... Heb 12:9

An unborn child in its mother's womb is oblivious to the reality of a larger world outside of the confinement that is its home. That world, though unseen and unknown by the unborn, is very real and in various ways directly impacts its normal growth and development.

This I believe is but one metaphor for the reality of the experience of humans in the 'womb' we call the world. There is a physical world, but I believe and the Bible teaches that there is also an unseen world, a larger spiritual reality.

In our daily lives, we wade through a sea of unseen things that are real: viruses, electrons, dust, radio waves etc. In the same way, the spiritual world is unseen to the natural eye, but generates many invisible and unknown forces that directly shape our perspectives and experiences. Those forces are real, even though science may choose to question or dismiss their reality because of the inability to provide rational explanations for their existence.

It is important to remember that most of the knowledge we now take for granted was veiled from the understanding of generations past, because they did not have the means to study, measure and quantify various phenomenon as we now can. Ultraviolet rays, microorganisms, genetic coding, electricity, gravity, the atom, etc., have always been present. They did not miraculously appear when science developed the means to document and articulate their existence. In the same way, we cannot and should not emphatically presume that we know all there is to know about the world around us, or the world *within* us. Science and scientific enquiry works well for things in the natural, tangible, physical realm that can be observed or measured, but will consistently fall short into enquiries regarding the spiritual realm for reasons we are about to explore.

We have stated that there is a world that exists beyond our physical world, but because we live in a physical world, it is easy to believe that what we see is the only reality. Our familiarity with the world around us typically comes through our five senses. This has led many to believe that a person is only the physical expression that can be experienced with our senses and many become imprisoned in this partial reality.

The bible, however, takes a very different view. It teaches that man (the male and female expression of humans) is made in the image of God.[6] Man is *not* a god, but rather a reflection of the very nature of God Himself. The Bible further teaches that God

---

[6]   Gen. 1:26, 27, 9:6

is a spirit.[7] An understanding of this idea is foundational to the remainder of our discussions, for if God is a spirit and man is made in His image, then man must also be a spirit! The body of man therefore, is a merely a container to express in the physical realm what man really is in actuality – a spirit.

This same God, the God of the bible is also called the "... Father of spirits".[8]

The Hebrew word 'father' means the originator or transmitter of anything.[9] In these two passages then, we are able to understand that God *is* a spirit and that He is the source or origination of *all* other spirits.

So what is a spirit? Based on the Strongs concordance, the Hebrew language uses three different words to define what spirit means, and each definition adds to our understanding of the concept:

- Strong's H7307 (ruwach)- an unaccountable or uncontrollable impulse; a living breathing being in man and animals; departing at death, disembodied being; temper anger and
- Strong's G4151 (pneuma)- a human soul that has left the body; the disposition or influence which fills and governs the mind, will and emotions of anyone; the source of any power, affection, emotion, desire etc.

---

[7] John 4:24

[8] Heb 12:9

[9] Strong's G3962

- Strong's H178('owb)- called a familiar spirit, the spirit of a dead one, ghost.

On the basis of the above and specifically in relation to humans, a spirit is first and foremost a *person*, the living breathing being *in* a man that is separate from but intertwined with the soul, that can depart from the body at death, becoming disembodied. For the body ceases to live when the spirit departs from it[10], while the spirit, made in the image of God, is eternal and continues to exist.

A spirit is also the *source or origin of various attributes or impulses.* The bible teaches that God does not just love, God *is* love.[11] He is a person who is also the original source of all power, good desires and so forth, but He has infused some of these qualities into other spirits He has created and has given them a will.

Joy, peace, patience, self control, kindness, gentleness, grace, compassion, godly wisdom etc., are positive spiritual attributes or manifestations of the nature of God who is the Supreme 'good' spirit. Though these attributes cannot be seen with the natural eye, for we cannot know the motive of an act, they can be experienced *within* a person and expressed *through* them. His nature, imbibed by people and cultivated through an act of their wills, would eventually cause these qualities to be expressed in the person's life. Bitterness, anger, unforgiveness, hatefulness, lack of control, deceitfulness, malice and so forth are negative, or

---

[10] James 2:26

[11] 1 John 4:8

ungodly spiritual qualities and we know that these undesirable qualities can also be cultivated or developed in a person's life through a variety of means. It is because God has given spirits the ability to make *choices* that the predominant qualities that a person develops in life influences how their spirit develops. Therefore, how a person's spirit develops determines what they express, either in or out of a body.

Let's state that again: a living person can, through acts of their will, influence what their spirit becomes and manifests or can manifest the attributes of other spirits. It seems that spirits cannot change their character after they have left the body! We have also seen spirits described as urges, impulses and anger and we will explore this aspect of them at a later time.

The categories of spirits created by God are each different in terms of their purpose and function:

Angels

The scriptures teach that angels are also spirits.[12] They do not have a physical body although many scriptures show that they can manifest physically to humans.

Angels fall into two categories- fallen and holy. As stated earlier, the bible teaches that satan and one third of the angels in heaven utilized their will to sin against God and were cast out.[13]

This group of fallen angels is incapable of expressing any *genuinely* godly spiritual attributes. Their spirits were permanently

---

12   Psalm 104:4, Heb 1:7
13   Rev. 12:9

distorted or perverted because of their disobedience. This is why everything they express is a distortion or perversion of what is good and true. The remaining two thirds of the angels function in the kingdom of God in various capacities.

Angels are obviously different spiritual beings than other spirits in terms of ability, knowledge, strength and purpose. Although they are stronger, smarter and more powerful than men, they were created to serve God and man, in various capacities and under *God's* direction. The fallen angels serve *themselves* and advance their own agenda under satan, the devil; as self service is the hallmark of sin.

Human

Man is unique among the other spirits created by God and is different from other created spirits in that man is made in the image of God. The bible speaks of no other created being in this way. The spirit of man, the man himself (his intellect, emotions, personality and will), was made to have a complementary physical container (body) that holds his spirit, allowing him to manifest and receive and give input into both the *physical and spiritual worlds*. This specific design of man has major implications for our existence in this realm as we shall explore later.

A final word here for those who may have grown up without a parent(s) in their lives for whatever reason, lament their absence and feel that they may have been deprived somehow, know that your parent(s) were the means by which the container was made for who you really are. You are a spirit and God is your true Father; the Father of who you truly are. You are not your body, you merely have one. God is ready, willing and able to abundantly supply far more than your absent earthly parent(s) ever could have, if He is given the opportunity.

Animals

Have a different kind of spirit than men or angels and are not made in the image of God. During the course of creation, animals were spoken into existence.[14] It is as thought the general breath of God brought animal life into being in a detached way. When God created man He intimately made contact with his form and breathed His concentrated essence into the container He had shaped. This is this singular fact that nullifies the theory of evolution from a biblical perspective. Man is not his physical body, but man is a spirit. The spirit of man and the spirit of animals are not fashioned in the same way, so the two cannot have a common ancestry.

Again animals *have* a spirit, but man *is* a spirit.

---

[14]   Gen 1: 24-25

CHAPTER THREE

The Creation and Fall of Man

"... the serpent deceived me and I ate." Gen 3:13

Science has no explanation for the existence of the human spirit as mentioned in the preceding chapter. In truth it does not have a cohesive explanation for the complexities of the human body, consciousness or thought. Evolution cannot explain what life is or how it came to be. It can theorize or hypothesize, but it is important to remember that evolution is still a theory; it is not a fact, as many teach and would like to have us believe. This may be a good place to briefly address the so called 'building blocks' of life.

In their endless search for the origins of "life", the scientific community often points to the presence of water, amino acids and other chemical compounds as indicators of the 'building blocks' of life. It doesn't matter if the search takes them to Mars, asteroid samples or other planets. But if these tangible compounds are in fact "building blocks" of life, then why do we die? Is it not true that every biologic or chemical compound that was present the nanosecond before a person exhales for the last time, is present *after* they exhale? Is it not clear that these things do not *give* life at all, but are in fact *given* life and an ability to function by another unseen force?

The Bible however, is emphatic in its declaration of how man came to be. It states that man was simply *created*. The following points have been made before, but for the sake of emphasis they are stated again. God *made* man in His image and after His likeness.[15] The word image means resemblance.[16] If man was made in the resemblance of God and if God is an eternal spirit, then man must also be an eternal spirit. This also means that man is *not* his body— he simply *has* a body and it also means that man will never die. The temporal part of man was only made to exist for a period of time in the dimension of time, but the spirit lives forever beyond time! On an intuitive level people know this, for He has put eternity in our hearts![17]

God formed man[18] (the body or container of the spirit) from the dust of the ground and God breathed into his nostrils the breath of life and man became a living soul[19] - (that which breathes, the inner being of man, the man himself, emotions, passion.) Therefore, man has a dual nature, the physical and the

---

[15]   Gen 1:27
[16]   Strong's H6754 (tselem)
[17]   Eccles. 3:11
[18]   Gen. 2:7
[19]   Strong's H5315 (nephesh)

spiritual which comprises the spirit and the soul (mind, will and emotions)!

After creating man, God commanded the man to be fruitful and multiply, exercise dominion over and subdue every other created thing in the world.[20] This command would include both the visible and invisible worlds as we shall see shortly. This singular act by God in creating man the way He did, made man unique in creation. With his body, man has a means of making contact with the material world, but because he is a spirit, he is also able to have influence in and receive things from the unseen spirit realm.

The Hebrew word for father that we defined above also means 'one who has infused his *own* spirit into another and is able to regulate and govern their minds'. So, consider then that when God made man and breathed into his nostrils, God infused his own spirit into man and intended to have that man exercise control and dominion in the physical realm, *while being regulated by the spirit of God in the man.* This is a key idea to grasp; the spirit of man is the place where man and God were to meet; a place for that man to commune with God, and to have God as a regulator of *all* of his activities while in the earth realm. Additionally, man was also given a free will, the right to choose not to cooperate with God; for true love or obedience cannot be forced!

Man was to be a representative of God's heavenly kingdom in the earth, carrying out the wishes of the King (God) and subduing everything in creation for His glory.

Remember too, that the devil had already sinned in heaven, was cast down to the earth and was present at the time of creation

---

[20] Gen. 1:28

and the commissioning of man who was to be God's representative in the earth.

Most of us are familiar with the story of what happened next. The bible teaches that the serpent was the slyest, craftiest of all the animals and made deceptive statements to the woman. Notice the spirit (influence) that initiated this dialogue aligned itself with the animal that was most like itself. Here we are able to see the deceiver at work in the background, using the spirit of an unseen force to influence the spirit of an animal. Through these means, he was able to make suggestions that 'opened up the mind' of the woman to a viewpoint she had not previously considered. A viewpoint, I might add that was contrary to the mandate they had already been given by God; a viewpoint focused on *self*!

All sins originate from the altered perspectives of men.

All sins are simply a twist if you will, of the normal, acceptable or entrenched standards imposed by God. When the suggestion appealed to her mind and emotions, she used her will to override a spiritual directive she and her husband had been given, which was to *have dominion over animals*. The biblical definition of the act of sin is to miss the mark, to fail to uphold the basic standard set by God as the guideline for human behavior. The most immediate consequence of their sin was a severing or a separation of their spiritual connection with God. That is what death is, separation *not* cessation. One does not cease to exist when one sins; one simply ceases to be connected!

This separation from having God's nature and influence infused into the spirit of man and God being a regulator of mans thoughts, explains every subsequent consequence. This allowed two opposing systems of governance to exist in the earth, one from below and the other from above. One driven by a desire to do God's will as He leads and the other to satisfy one's own desires for one's own benefit. One led by the Spirit, the other by the senses; one with temporal benefits, the other with eternal rewards. To this very day, many do not understand what has been lost and spend all their energies trying to accumulate benefits in the dimension of time, while ignoring the realities of eternity, to their detriment.

This also helps us to understand what the concept of being born a sinner means. Through that singular act of disobedience they renounced their right to be Kingdom citizens. Adam and Eve's sin and the severing of their spiritual connection with God meant that all of their offspring born after this event would now be born outside of the kingdom of God.

They now existed in, and their offspring would later be born into a state of separation from God, incapable of being regulated by Him from within. That *state* is called sin. So we now recognize that there is the *state* of sin into which **all** people are born and then there are *acts* of sin, things people do that fall below God's standard. Therefore, although actions can be sinful, a person is also called a sinner because of *where* he was born (outside of the Kingdom). This is why Jesus told Nicodemus "… you must be born again."[21] It is because of this state of sin that people cannot have their hearts regulated by God. It is because of the state of sin that people instinctively do wrong things. The proclivity to miss

---

[21]   John 3:7

the standards of God is inherent in **every** person born outside of the kingdom of God. It is also why no 'morally upright' person by mans standards is considered to be a good or righteous person by God's standards. We were **all** born in sin. The acts we may commit to express our citizenship in the state of sin may vary, but make no mistake *all* have sinned.[22]

Another consequence of sin is that man was plunged into spiritual darkness. The bible teaches that the spirit of man is the candle of the Lord.[23] When man was spiritually connected to God, he was alive and full of light, like a lamp plugged into a socket. Man was filled with the glory and mind of God. God was able to speak to the man within, spirit to spirit. All of mans ideas, urges and desires were pure and reflective of God's nature and desires, and they were heard *within* the man, in his spirit. Man was designed by God to be led from above, not from below; to be led by what was unseen, not by what was seen. There was no need for speech heard with the physical ears. This is why the enemy had to speak to the woman audibly through the serpent. He had no place in the spirit or soul of man at that time.

After the man sinned, the lamp was disconnected from its source, the light within went out and immediately the spirit of man was filled with darkness, an evil called the 'spirit of the world'.[24] So, the spirit of the world hijacked the system of communication that God had with man. It started to communicate with man the

---

[22] Rom. 3:23

[23] Prov. 20:27

[24] 1 Cor. 2:12

way God did, *within* the man, through thoughts, ideas, dreams, urges and so on.

Let's emphasize that again, for all those who have scoffed at the idea of God talking to His children and seem to have difficulty both believing and understanding *how* He does it, the answer is that God talks to His children *the same way* the 'spirit of the world' speaks to all those born outside of the kingdom of God, through thoughts, ideas and promptings of the spirit *within* the person. Only God's modes of communication originate from above *not* from below!

God, who was displaced from His rightful place *within* the man, now had to speak audibly to the physical ear of man to communicate with him for the first time. This process is confirmed through multiple examples throughout Old Testament scriptures and He still does with unbelievers today. This is why preachers are needed. Man now has to hear the truth firstly with his physical ears and then use his mind, combined with faith, to believe in Jesus so that his spirit can be born again. Once born again, God can communicate with man spirit to spirit again. In fact, this is how God the Father communicated with Jesus during His earthly ministry; spirit to spirit. Remember, Jesus was called the second Adam, He was spiritually alive and in constant communication with the Father within His spirit.[25] He physically and spiritually represented in the earth all the Adam was and could do before he fell.

---

[25] John 12:50

This also enables us to understand why Adam was afraid when he heard the sound of God walking in the garden.[26] For the first time he had to use his physical ears to hear God and he had to use his physical mouth to speak with Him. Since his spiritual connectivity to God was severed by sin and he was no longer useful or qualified to represent the kingdom of God in the earth, he was put out of the Garden of Eden. A simple analogy would be that if a limb were cut off a tree, although it still appears to be alive it is no longer connected to the tree, the source of life and cannot express the nature of the tree and bear fruit, rendering it useless.

Since the spirit is the place where man is designed to be influenced and controlled, Adams sin transferred legal authority for rule and control to the devil. It is this spirit that has so entrenched the idea of 'self' in the human experience that among the first words a child utters is, "mine". It is through the ideas of 'mine' and 'more', that the devil has seduced and influenced subsequent generations of men to build a 'kingdom' that would oppose the establishment of God's kingdom in the earth. He does this by the thoughts, feelings urges and impulses he stirs in the hearts of men. This also creates a conundrum for the believer because they are now able to receive instructions from two sources, above *and* below. Having a renewed spirit allows one to receive directives from God in one's spirit, but it doesn't automatically negate the influence of the spirit of the world in a person's mind. The believer is now put in the position of having to learn what the bible says, develop a personal relationship with God and then constantly choose to do what is right before Him and modify

---

[26] Gen. 3:8

their thoughts and actions to align with its teachings. This takes time as one learns to overcome the habits and inclinations they learned before their spiritual rebirth. The struggle is real!

The simple message of the gospel of the Kingdom is that mankind was cut off from God by sin and Jesus came to give us the opportunity to be 'born again' spiritually, to regain our spiritual citizenship and to reconnect us to the Father to re-establish the work of extending His Kingdoms influence in this realm. We do this by learning to exercise the authority He has given us. God's kingdom is firstly a spiritual kingdom that must be built by His citizens, spiritually alive to Him and able to commune with Him in spirit and truth.[27] They must be able to receive and carry out His instructions in the modus operandi of His kingdom, spirit to spirit.

Yielding to the influence of a spirit gives that spirit control and authority in the area of life where the person gave in. This is the principle behind the story of the fall of man and it is true in our experience with spirits today.

---

[27] John 4:26

CHAPTER FOUR

The Significance of A Body

... a body you have prepared for me. Heb. 10:5 NKJV

So far we have touched on several important truths as taught in the bible. Firstly, that there is a God. Secondly, that this God has created all things. There is nothing that exists, seen or unseen that was not created by God. Among His creations are various classes of spirit beings, each of whom were made for different purposes. However, a little clarification is needed here, for God did not create evil. He created spirits with free will, some of whom chose to deviate from His will causing evil to come into existence!

It is also extremely important to understand that the *only* spirit being that was to be legitimately housed in a physical container (body) in the earth was the spirit of man. The body was designed to be the servant of the human spirit in the physical realm. It allows a nonphysical entity to make contact with and accomplish things in the physical world. Remember the principle is that the spirit of man was to receive instructions from God; man would then use his will to agree with God's desires and then use his body to manifest those desires in the physical realm. It is the hijacking of this principle that allows evil to manifest in the world.

Many have wondered why a good God would allow the acts of evil that people commit against each other to happen, but they do not understand fundamental spiritual principles. We have stated before that earth is the domain of *men*, not of God. So, if people choose to reject God, it is still the domain of men; we are still its stewards. Hopefully, we can now appreciate that when evil acts happen, it is not God's fault at all, but rather it is a consequence of mans abdication and **ignorance** of his true duties and responsibilities in the earth, while cooperating with forces that are against God. Consider that nobody ever asks the question of why God allows good in the world when *good* things happen! A better question then is why won't men co-operate with God so that evil won't manifest? No murder, rape, theft, war (just or unjust), abuse or any other evil happens without the body of a person acting on certain ideas. The common denominator in injustice, perversion and atrocities is **man**, not God.

We must remember too that death is not the end of the existence of man; so even after an act has been committed and a person has died and seemingly gotten away with the act, they haven't. God has already set a time to judge **all** men, for all the acts committed while in the body. [28] The devil knows this, but his operatives specialize in deception, hiding the truth about God from man, hiding the truth about who man is from the man

---

[28]   2 Cor. 5:10

himself, and then using perversion (twisting) of God's word and laws to seduce man into ungodly acts.

It is the spirit that gives life to the body.[29] The body is nothing without the spirit. That unseen, animating force called 'life' is carried in the blood.[30] When blood ceases to flow and life is no longer carried, either to a part of or all of the body, death occurs, either in that part or in the entire body. Once physical death occurs, the spirit of the person leaves the body. That person now becomes a spirit without a body; a disembodied spirit. This highlights the fact that the body is temporal and ultimately disposable. It is the lesser part of who we are, but the systems of the world have gotten many to believe it is the most important. This is why people spend so much of their resources accentuating aspects of their bodies, to the neglect of the eternal part of them; their spirit!

The only Spirit that can give life to a dead body is the Spirit of God, because He is the source of life. Spirits therefore are unable to use dead bodies. The only spirit that can cause physical matter to manifest from nothing is God. This one truth highlights the reason for the copious amounts of spiritual activity in the natural realm; spirits trapped in this realm are vying for entrance into human bodies.

A man is only useful to God in the earth as long as he has a body. Once the body has been discarded by physical death, man has lost his usefulness in the physical realm.

---

[29]   John 6:63

[30]   Lev 17:11

A man is only useful to spirits as long as he has a body.

So again, the sole purpose of the body is to manifest the mind or desires of the unseen in the natural realm. The thoughts, ideas and concepts that originate in the unseen world of the spirit are manifested in the natural world by mans using his mind and body. We are creators in the physical realm as we are influenced by the spiritual. Although this ability was initially only to be used for good, it is also true for the manifestation evil as well. Once that manifestation has occurred, there are usually rewards associated. Rewards from the spirit world are based on a simple principle: the system whose agenda you advance rewards you.[31] For example, a man receives an idea or spiritual instruction. He develops the idea into a physical tangible 'thing' that can be shared with others in the natural realm. The man does this by using his faith in the idea to create or manifest it. The reward for his efforts would be determined by whose cause he advanced and the impact of his efforts. Satan's reward systems revolve around the temporal and the sensual: money, physical pleasure, the adulation of others in the world.[32] This is the reason why certain groups of individuals are rewarded lavishly by the *world*; they either create the vehicle through which demonically inspired ideas can more easily reach the masses or they embody and promote specific ungodly ideals that influence others. In essence, certain individuals allow themselves to be used to propagate ideas or products that entrench the devils ability to exert even greater control over the minds

---

[31]   Luke 4:6

[32]   1 John 2:16

and the wills of men, and then the world system that he owns, rewards them for it. The devil even boasted to Jesus that he (the devil) gives power to those whom he chooses. [33] This is also why, generally speaking, the wealthiest and most popular people in the world are usually the most morally and spiritually bankrupt, and ironically, when they die, their net worth is usually published, when what really matters is not what they left behind, but what was sent ahead, into eternity! For we shall be alive *out* of the body far longer than we were alive *in* it!

Conversely, in God's kingdom the rewards of advancing His cause in this world are temporal and spiritual. Skepticism, abuse, ridicule and persecution emanate *from the world* because it opposes the things of God, but the rewards He gives will last for all eternity.[34] Very often, if a true believer amasses a great fortune he is ridiculed by those both within and outside of the church. The devil simply does not want those who are actively opposing him in the earth to have the resources to do so. Again, it is foolish to expect the worlds systems to embrace a work that directly opposes it. Therefore, the body is central both to God and the devils purposes for man to manifest their respective wills in the earth.

Man's sin during the fall, affected all of physical and spiritual creation. It is why the incarnation had to occur. Jesus had to, in His **body**, cooperate with the plan of God in the earth! The work Jesus was to do could not be performed in the spiritual realm only, since the sin that caused man to fall was *physical* with spiritual

---

[33]   Luke 4:6

[34]   Matt. 25: 31-40

implications. His physical body also allowed Him to teach, preach and exercise authority over spirits in this realm. Jesus' physical body satisfied the physical requirements of sacrifice, that atoned mans sins and also transferred spiritual authority back to man. This allows the man who is in right standing with God through his relationship with Jesus, to have authority over the devil, while still in the earth. With his relationship with God restored, man can now be infused with the spirit of His creator to manifest **His** wishes in the physical realm, as was the original intent. The only problem is that there is opposition in the physical realm, through the devil working in the bodies of others to manifest his evil agenda.

This may be why Jesus commanded His disciples to love their enemies. He understood the extent to which man was spiritually ignorant and that the physical body was just being used to advance the devils agenda. This would cause one man without spiritual insight to hate another man who opposed him. But as Paul said "...we do not wrestle with flesh and blood, but against principalities and powers....[35]

It is mans cooperation with thoughts, ideas and suggestions that oppose God's agenda that has created diverse cultures that are religious, but anti-God. The spirit that is at the heart of these anti-God agendas has expertly infiltrated mans spirit and then used the body to get man to express the vile, profane and perverse by God's standards. Now, what is considered vile, profane or perverse is based on the standards that God established to govern man's actions, not on constantly shifting cultural perspectives. The

---

[35] Eph. 6:12

fact that the spirit that has deceived man into committing these acts, knowing that man is largely ignorant of what is happening and will be judged and punished for his complicity, is even more despicable.

This may also be an appropriate place to briefly consider what are called mental illnesses. We have established the fact that what a person believes becomes true to *them* based on the faith principle. We have also mentioned that urges, impulses etc., can originate from spirits that can gain entrance into the bodies of the living. *Most* mental disorders therefore will originate from at least one of those two categories. A belief in thoughts and ideas that are untrue, lie at the foundation of what I would call 'thought based disorders' like: anxiety, phobias, body dysmorphic syndrome and some of the depressive conditions for example. This is easily demonstrated when a person believes something for which there is contrary objective evidence. So if a person believes that a tomato *is* or can become a pumpkin, they have a delusion or 'thought based disorder'. These are usually corrected by the person learning to believe the truth; for only belief in the truth can extinguish the raging fire of a lie.

Most addictions, personality disorders, impulse driven disorders, psychoses and other conditions that affect a person's *will* and compels them to behave in specific ways, originate from other spirits. So, those who claim to see things or hear voices telling them to commit certain acts that they are helpless against, for instance, fall into this group. Medications can help to manage the symptoms of these conditions, but because the problem is spiritual, the only solution is spiritual as well! This is why we must try to arm ourselves with knowledge of the truth.

So, when man opposes the thoughts, ideas and suggestions of the spirits in this world, those spirits are unable to advance their agenda. The degree to which a man gives in to the ideas and suggestions that spirits have made, is the same degree to which the physical representation of good or evil will manifest in that person and in the earth.

CHAPTER FIVE

A World of Spirits

"... do not believe every spirit, but test the spirits to see whether they are from God ...." 1John 4:1

As highlighted in previous chapters, included in the list of creatures man was initially commissioned to have control over was the devil and the angels who fell with him. We have established however, that man was tricked and control of the earth was transferred to the devil, enabling him to influence it from the unseen realm by influencing man's spirit.

We have stated briefly that spirits are of different kinds with different purposes and functions. Although this is not intended to be an exhaustive study of angels, demons and other spirits, in this chapter we will explore the different types of spirits in this realm more closely, starting with angels.

Angels

For millennia, angels have fascinated various cultures. We have already stated that they will fall into two categories: those who did not sin and those cast out with the devil. While the bible does not teach specifically on angels, we are able to glean some knowledge based on references made about them in the Bible.

Although no passage states specifically how angels were created, we do know that God created them by the breath of his mouth.[36] We also know that they are large in number, and in his vision John the apostle sees them as "...ten thousand times ten thousand and thousands of thousands" and these are only those found around the throne of God during that particular experience. [37] Jesus once stated that he could have summoned more than twelve legions of angels (more than 72,000) if he wanted to be delivered from those who intended to crucify Him.[38]

We also know that they have their own language although they are able to communicate with men in the languages of earth.[39]

Angels have limited knowledge. [40] Although they have superior knowledge and intelligence compared to humans, they do not know everything. Angels for example do not know when Jesus will return and there are matters they desire to look into concerning Gods relationship with man. Paul states that the devil would not have crucified Jesus if they knew that His

---

[36]   Psalm 33:6

[37]   Heb. 12:22, Rev. 5:11

[38]   Matt. 26:53

[39]   1 Cor. 13:1

[40]   Matt. 24:36, 1 Pet. 1:12

death was the beginning of the end of their dominion in the earth.[41] Additionally, although angels are exceedingly intelligent, I am unaware of any scripture references that suggest that they have creative abilities like God or man. After all, the devil works *through* man to manifest his work in the world!

Angels have a different kind of body than humans.[42] Scriptures are replete with stories of angelic appearances and visitations. The bodies of angels can take on a physical form and have physical properties, but they also have supernatural qualities as well. They can appear and disappear at will without physical hindrances and do not seem to be confined to the earth realm.

Abraham was visited by angels who displayed the normal attributes of humans by sitting, eating and talking with him. Lot was visited in Sodom by two angels who stayed in his house and then destroyed Sodom and the surrounding cities because of their sin. Daniel was put in a den of lions but testified that an angel shut the lion's mouth.[43] Peter was awakened in jail and supernaturally led out by an angel. The writer of Hebrews stated that even in the church age, some entertained angels in their homes. Angels can obviously look and act like humans, but they are only in that form in the earth realm for a short period of time to carry out a specific assignment.

There is no scripture that implies that angels can reproduce. The scriptures seem to suggest that the capacity to reproduce was only given to those with physical bodies, men and animals. This

---

[41]   1 Cor. 2:8

[42]   Gen. 19:1, 1King 19:5, Heb. 13:2, Act 12:6, etc

[43]   Dan. 6:22

seems logical since only limited amounts of men and animals were made during creation; they would have to reproduce to increase their numbers on the earth. In addition, the law of a creature reproducing after its own kind seems restricted to men and animals; a general principle in the bible is that like begets like. Humans, made in part from the dust of the ground and angels, are two different kinds of creation and are unlikely to be able to produce offspring, as some have speculated has happened.

Angels can appear in dreams and visions.[44] Dreams only occur in sleep. Visions are visual experiences that a person may have while fully or partially awake. While dreams are viewed as perfectly normal, in our culture, visions are not. They are called hallucinations, restricted primarily to experimental or recreational drug users and those characterized as mentally ill. Even in our modern age there are so many instances of non-drug induced visions occurring, that all of them cannot be a result of mental illness.

In the bible, men and women frequently received instruction and directions from angels through dreams and visions.

Angels are powerful beings.[45] The first story recounts how in one night the angel of the Lord killed one hundred and eighty five thousand enemy soldiers. The other shows how they can be present but unseen to the natural eye, in great numbers. They are able to fly to the aid of, fight on behalf of and protect God's people as He chooses. In Psalm 91 it tells us that God has delegated certain of His angels to protect His children. This may

---

[44]   Gen 31:11, Matt 2:13

[45]   2 Kings 19:35, 2 Kings 6:17

be where the concept of guardian angels comes from. The book of Revelations shows many depictions of phenomenal acts being performed by angels.

Angels have different roles, messenger, warrior, service etc. The very large numbers of angels must imply that there are many different roles for these angels to fulfill. Gabriel is entrusted with many important messages, but there are other messenger angels.[46] Angels showed up to minister to Jesus several times throughout His ministry and are credited with a whole host of other events in the history of the church.[47]

Michael seems to be head of the army in heaven, but there are other angels in military roles in God's kingdom as well.[48]

Angels do not receive the worship of men.[49] This is a fundamental difference between demons and God's angels; demons crave the worship of man.

Angels can execute the judgment of God.[50] One of the most common examples is found in Exodus 12:23, when the 'angel of death' killed the first born males and animals in Egypt during the first Passover. Revelations 16 recount many acts of judgment carried out by the angels of God particularly in the last days.

Angels can sin. Satan's forceful expulsion from heaven along with one third of the angels is ample proof that angels have free will- the right to choose good or evil and they can exercise that

---

[46]   Dan. 8:16, 9:21, Luke 1:19

[47]   Acts 12

[48]   Rev. 12:7

[49]   Rev. 22:8-9

[50]   Matt. 13:41

will against God. However, because angels have seen more of who God is and what He can do they also have greater consequences attached to their sin. Since they have more knowledge, they do not receive forgiveness for sins.

Angels do not die. Spirits have some of the essence and nature of God in them. One of God's attributes is that He is eternal. Since angels and humans are spirits, they are eternal. For this reason they cannot be destroyed, but they can be contained and restricted in time and space. It is for this reason God created hell and the lake of fire as the eternal resting place of all disobedient spirits.[51]

Physical death is not the end of one's existence; rather, it is the beginning of a never-ending existence in another realm.

Fallen angels

Fallen angels will have the same qualities in their spiritual bodies as holy angels do. They vary in power and ability, but are able to do everything that godly angels are able to do, however, their motivation is to serve themselves and oppose God. Their knowledge and use of their abilities has been twisted (perverted) by sin. They do not require constant use or control of a body. They may enter a body on special occasions when something specific must be accomplished and nothing could be left to chance. The best example is when the devil entered Judas.[52]

---

[51]   Matt. 25: 41

[52]   Luke 22:3

Some are held in bondage until judgment.[53] They are organized with ranks. Paul makes it clear that the struggles we have in this world is not against people but rather unseen spiritual forces that rank in power.[54] Daniel makes reference to an angel of God meeting resistance from a spirit in the devils kingdom called the Prince of Persia and he speaks of another called the Prince of Greece.

In Mark 5, Jesus healed a man who was possessed with many demons. Immediately prior to casting out the demons they asked not to be sent out of the area; a request with which Jesus complied. These are examples of fallen angels influencing geographic areas.[55]

In Matthew 4:8-9 and Luke 4:5-6, the devil told Jesus that he would give Him "all the kingdoms of the world" if He would bow down and worship him. This scriptures among many others shows that the devil presides as sovereign over the cultures, politics and economies of the nations of the world. We must note in the above example that Jesus did not contest the devil having possession of the power and authority that controls and influences the world, but he is still called a liar and the originator of lies.[56] This implies that most of what he encourages the world to believe is simply not true *because* he deceives the whole world.[57]

Fallen angels also can pervert the creative abilities of man.

---

[53] 2 Pet. 2:4, Jude 1:6

[54] Eph. 6:12

[55] Dan. 10:13, 20

[56] John 8:44

[57] Rev. 12:9

We have already stated that because man is created in God's image and likeness, God has endowed man with certain abilities that other creatures in creation do not have. Among the unique capabilities of man is the ability to see things in his mind. If man is able to clearly see a thing in his mind and believe it, he can make it happen. This is the faith principle mentioned before. It is this principle that the devil uses to inject thoughts and imaginations into a man's mind to enable the man to create things and schemes that entangle and ensnare other men in order to offend God.

Disembodied Spirits

There are different kinds of disembodied spirits and ghosts are one of them.[58]

There are many who believe in the existence of ghosts, but those who believe often do not know what ghosts are, or what they are capable of. The bible supports the view that ghosts are real. You may recall that each of the definitions of spirit we reviewed in an earlier chapter included some aspect of the human spirit. That ghosts are human spirits without a body is clear from scripture.

In Matthew 14, the disciples saw a figure walking on the sea toward their boat and were fearful saying it is a ghost (which means apparition).[59] Jesus did not say they were foolish for believing in such things, but rather told them not to be afraid because it was Him *not* a ghost. In the other passage (Luke 24), Jesus has already risen from the dead. He appeared in a closed room where

---

[58]   Matt. 14:26-27, Luke 24:37-39

[59]   Strong's G5326- phantasma

the disciples were and they were afraid thinking they were seeing a ghost. He said "...touch me for a spirit (pneuma) does not have flesh and bones." We have already seen that 'pneuma' is the Greek word for a human soul that has left the body: it is also the disposition or influence that can fill and *govern* the soul of *anyone*; it is the source of *any* power, affection, emotion or desire.

We learn several things from these passages. Firstly, that Jesus knew that ghosts were real and that they can take on an appearance that allows them to be seen (phantasm), but they do not have a physical body. In addition, they are human spirits of unbelievers, without bodies and confined to the earth realm. They can enter and control others causing desires, emotions etc., or can give them power to do certain things. It is this understanding that explains the apparent supernatural power or knowledge that some humans appear to have. These ghosts are only able to gain access to a human body by exploiting spiritual laws humans are unaware of.

Not all ghosts will be destructive or ill intentioned, because remember they are the spirits of the departed. They will not want to hurt those they love and may even try to 'protect' and help them if they can. Ghosts become problematic when they have perverse desires and appetites and want to continue their existence in another person's body.

Another type of disembodied spirit is the "unclean spirit".[60] The bible speaks specifically about unclean spirits many times. Matthew 12:43 states that "… when the unclean spirit has come out of a man he walks through dry places, seeking rest and finds

---

[60] Matt. 12:43, 12:45, Mark 1:26-27, Mark 3:11

none." These spirits in particular seem to be tormented and in need a body, because of the inclination they have to express their perverse desires. The word unclean is from the Greek (Strong's G169- akathartos), which means unclean in *thought and life*, morally impure) and helps us understand that this is the disembodied spirit of a really wicked person. This spirit in particular seems more tormented than other disembodied spirits. Its goal is to find ease, rest from its torment. It seems to have a great appetite to commit the sins it did when alive in its own body, but having died, it wants to express those same desires through others in order to find ease from its torment. When it does not find any ease, it leaves the body it has accessed and wanders. One if its characteristics, is the excessive immoral indulgences or acts of violence it drives it occupants to engage in. There are those with various proclivities, addictions etc. who may seem fine for a while and then revert to their previous habits with unexplained ferocity. This spirit in particular explains this cyclical behavior.

Another important point to note is that spirits are not made of matter, and consequently an infinite number can inhabit one host. It may be easier to picture this if one thinks of spirits as a form of energy that exists in different frequencies, in the same way that the different frequencies of musical instruments in an orchestra can co-exist in one room! In Mark 5: 9, Jesus encounters a demonically possessed man, who was tormented day and night. Jesus drives the spirits out of him and he is restored to wholeness, but the spirits enter a herd of pigs and approximately 2,000 of them rush into the sea and die. This must mean that at a minimum, there were 2,000 spirits in the formerly possessed man; one man, multiple spirits. This also brings to mind the idea of those with so called "multiple personality disorders" that was mentioned in an earlier chapter, for how can a person given one spirit by God, manifest more than one personality *unless* there is more than one personality *in* them? This teaches us two things: firstly that spirits can enter the bodies of animals, but humans are a preferable host for reasons explained above. Secondly, when the host dies, or the spirits are driven out, they will become disembodied again and look for another host, for spirits do not die!

Familiar spirits are another type of disembodied spirit, that enables the person it possesses to have the ability to evoke the spirit of other dead people, usually in an effort to tell the future or to gain information otherwise unknown;[61] a practice called necromancy. While there are charlatans in all spheres of human influence, there are actually those who function with this ability under the influence of these spirits.

Demons

The bible makes several references to demons, a group of spirits with the power to fulfill specific assignments. These would be considered the 'special forces' in the devils organization.

Let's consider the Greek definitions of demons to get a more comprehensive understanding of what they are and what they do:

- Strong's H7700 (shed)- devils who allow themselves to be worshipped.

---

[61]   Lev. 19:31, 1 Sam. 28:9, Isaiah 8:19)

- Strong's G1140 (daimonion)- evil spirits or the messengers and ministers of the devil. The divine power, a spirit, inferior to God, superior to men.
- Strong's G1142 (daimon)- a god or goddess, an inferior deity, an evil spirit.
- Strongs H8163 (sai'yr)- resembling he-goats, inhabiting deserts. Demons then are fallen angels <u>or</u> human spirits who allow themselves to be worshipped or who serve the devil in various capacities.

Any disembodied spirit can be categorized as a demon once it has been enlisted to carry out a specific assignment against a person or group of persons. This is the principle upon which casting curses works in the occult. When that person casts a 'spell', a spirit is enlisted to carry out specific acts against a person or group of persons.

While those who are spiritually dead (unbelievers) may be influenced, possessed or harassed by disembodied spirits (ghosts) predominantly, those who are productive believers will invariably be dealing with demons because of the conflict that now occurs between the two kingdoms. Once a person, born outside of the kingdom of God, has made a decision to receive the life that comes from accepting Jesus and being led from above, that person has committed 'spiritual treason' and is a threat to the advancement of the devils agenda in the earth.

Satan's objective is to destroy or neutralize the influence of the believer in "his" territory, as he sees it. It is also the reason why preachers, teachers and other ministers of the gospel may be relentlessly attacked and fall into sin. Once they have fallen into sin, perverse spirits or demons are assigned to take them down the path of grossly immoral acts or the preaching of heresy. Those ministers or preachers who have fallen into embarrassing sins or depravity are examples of this. Ignorance of this principle of *spiritual treason* has caused many believers to get frustrated in their faith, become nominal in their beliefs or to walk away from God when bad things happen. It is the targeting of believers by specialized unseen forces that underscores the point that spiritual warfare is real.

I would like to reiterate this point, most, if not all humans on this planet are influenced or possessed by various disembodied spirits, but believers in particular are harassed by demons (human or fallen angel spirits sent on a specific assignment to hinder or destroy them) in order to oppose the advancement of God's kingdom in the earth.

Since the devil has control of the unseen realm around man, he maintains that control by deception.[62] A part of the deception that has been perpetrated is to have a person believe that he (the devil) does not exist and/or that God is a stiff, judgmental law-giver who is waiting for us to step out of line so that he can destroy us. The latter view, which we have all heard is the exact opposite of the truth. The passage in Luke 9: 54-56 shows Jesus being disrespected and two of the disciples asking Him if they should call fire down from heaven to destroy the disrespectful. Jesus stated simply the motive and mission of God, which is not to destroy men's lives, but to save them.

---

[62]   Rev 12:9

As we review the roles of demons, consider that there is no ancient culture in which gods were not worshipped. The gods worshipped, the bible teaches were demons, stealing the worship only God deserves as the supreme creator.[63] This established cultural norms of spirit worship and the deceiving of men. This also explains their geographic influences. Different demons have different territorial influences.

God's rules and laws were given for the protection of men from the unseen world of evil spirits. This means that *every* spirit (every urge, every impulse or every idea) that is not sent directly from God with a message that is consistent with the principles of His kingdom, is coming from a deceiving spirit. Consider the implications of such a statement. This raises the question and quite possibly supplies the answer about the ubiquitous urges and impulses that arise in the living, seemingly without cause. If what we have learned so far about the nature of spirits is true, then it seems that it is the disembodied spirit who is able to account for uncontrollable or unaccountable impulses, temper and anger in those with bodies. Stated another way, it seems that uncontrollable impulses, urges or desires that arise within a person, without an obvious cause or explanation can be caused by a spirit other than the person's own spirit!

Every person who has ever lived has noticed inexplicable feelings, urges or desires of differing intensities at various times in their lives. Others also claim they always knew they had a certain proclivities. These people are ignorant of the fact that they can choose to accept or to resist giving into the feeling or

---

63   1 Cor. 10:20

desires. The person who yields to the urges and impulse of a spirit, invites or rather permits the influence of that spirit into themselves; this may eventually result in the person giving over control of an area of their lives to the causative spirit. That spirit will then continue to entice the person to engage in the activity that allows it to become a habit and eventually a personality trait. This is also why psychology is of limited use here and in similar mental illnesses, because one cannot use psychobabble to make spirits leave their host!

The truth of what was stated above is reinforced by the passage in Romans 6:16, which teaches that when a person places themselves at the disposal of sin or righteousness they will become a slave of what they chose to obey. Therefore a person who gives into and continues to practice kindness, patience and temperance will become that kind of person. The person who repeatedly gives into perverse urges, anger, drug use etc., will allow those spirits to control their lives and manifest these traits in their personality.

After the fall, God forbade man to have contact with the spirit realm on pain of death. That would not have been necessary if contact with other spirits was not possible. God knew that deceiving spirits would succeed in diluting and perverting the truth of who He is, why man was created and why man is incomplete without a relationship with God. He also knew that the infusion of ungodly ideas from the spirit realm would be the driving force that would eventually shape and influence evolving cultures in the world. Those influences would occur firstly in small communities and then larger territories and finally, globally. This is why men have always been driven to conquest, because they are tools to spread a particular "influence" beyond their borders, under the illusion of *self* attainment!

To combat the march of the kingdom of darkness in the world, God called a new people and created a new nation, Israel, to reintroduce the idea of who He was. God knew that yielding to the vices of seducing spirits in the lands where He was taking His people would cause them to degenerate into perverse advertisements of demonic ideology. He also knew that once *certain* demons became entrenched in men who were spiritually isolated from God there was no redemption for them. Very few if any, can try certain drugs and decide that they do not want it any more. Very few if any can enter a 'same sex' lifestyle and decide that they do not want to engage in it anymore and leave. Once the spirit associated with that choice enters, the occupant is rendered helpless and becomes controlled by that spirit. The person's ability to exercise free will is stifled, and they become driven to perform the desires of the spirit in them. They come to believe that the controlling spirit is who they are!!

We sometimes hear of those who committed vile or perverse acts saying they could not help themselves, or they heard voices telling them what to do. They are telling the truth! Since there was no release from the controlling spirit for the defiled before Christ, God's law stated that they had to be put to death. Death became the deterrent for God's people at that time, to ensure that those behaviors did not become a cultural norm, as they are today. It was a way to encourage the practice of self control, in order to teach people to resist urges and feelings in order to minimize the cancerous spread of abominable demonic ideology. In fact, one of the most fundamental things a good parent would try to teach their children is *not* to give in to every thought or feeling you have, but to think of the consequences of that action instead. The failure of so many to raise their children with this principle, explains the rampant confusion and social maladjustment seen in so many young people today!

As alluded to above, there were two basic groups of sin: those requiring appeasement (sacrifice) or those deserving of death. In the Old Testament Leviticus 20:27, the specific command was given to put to death those who had familiar spirits. Death was also commanded for adultery, blasphemy, worshipping other gods, homosexuality, incest, striking a parent, bestiality etc.[64] On the surface these instructions may seem barbaric to those with 21st century sensibilities. However, we must remember that we now accept socially that which was not accepted 50 years ago. Society's definitions of 'normal' have changed and a person who has the values towards sexuality and family that were esteemed 50 years ago would be called a small minded, bigot today.

The second problem that arises is that if man cooperates with ungodly spirits, the man legitimizes the actions of the spirit in the natural realm and knowingly or unknowingly aligns himself against God. This brings the man under the judgment of God and without repentance that one becomes doomed to hell, which was initially reserved *only* for rebellious angels. [65]

---

[64] Lev. 20:8- 15, 24:16

[65] Matt. 25:41

We must consider God's instructions in light of His unlimited knowledge and perspective. Additionally, we must remember that once man was separated from God, there was only one other pervasive spiritual influence in the world, that of the devil. It was and is God's desire to protect mankind from it.

CHAPTER SIX

After Death Then What

Wherefore, as by one man sin entered into the world, and death by sin; and so death passed upon all men, for that all have sinned. Rom 5:12 KJV

For the wages of sin is death, but the gift of God is eternal life through Jesus Christ our Lord. Rom 6:23 KJV

Very few things in life can conjure up fear as the thought or experience of impending death. This is primarily because many do not know what death is, nor do they know what lies beyond.

When a person enters this physical realm through birth, the first thing they do is inhale. This is reminiscent of Adams experience when God breathed His breath into the shaped ground, so that man would become a 'living soul'.[66] Whenever a person departs from this physical realm, the last thing they do is exhale. The experience we call life, is all that happens between those two

66   Gen. 2:7 KJV

breaths. Physical death is natural consequence of the exhalation of the animating life force in a man.

Remember that the very nature of man is that he *is* a spirit, has a soul and lives in a body. The body cannot survive without the spirit.[67] The life from the spirit that animated the body ceases to flow and the physical body made of matter dies. Instead of having a cohesive unit, we have a separation of the parts. Death of the physical body ultimately is due to sin. The process by which it manifests is due to age, trauma, disease or any other process that makes it impossible for the body to continue to contain the spirit.

Death is not the end of life. Physical death is the release of the spirit from the body and the beginning of an inescapable existence in another realm. If only people who commit suicide were aware of this fact.

There are many reports of people who have had what are termed near death experiences. The descriptions that many of the persons give who have had these experiences are consistent with the bibles views on the dual nature of man. They invariably describe being separated from their bodies, but they are still able to see the body. This supports the bibles view that the spirit of a man *is* the man, not the body. The body is merely a container for the spirit and allows man to make contact with the physical world around him. It also shows that the spirit has specific faculties like sight, hearing, memory, understanding, intellect and so on. There are many beliefs that people have concerning life after death and

---

[67] John 6:63 NIV

these beliefs are as diverse as the cultures in which they are found, but let's briefly explore what the bible teaches.

After being permanently separated from the body (death) a person can continue to exist in one of four states:

Heaven

In both the Old and New Testaments specific references are made to a place, unseen to the natural eyes, where God dwells with the angels. It is the place where God has centralized His power and has His throne. God, the bible teaches, is not the God of the dead but the living.[68] In this passage Jesus makes it clear that although the righteous dead are no longer in this realm they are very much alive. In Hebrews 12:1, we are reminded that unseen to our eyes are a great body of believers encouraging us to persevere in our faith.

When a believer in Jesus is separated from their body, they are instantaneously present with the Lord in heaven.[69] They have stepped out of the realm of time, with all of its constraints, into an eternity in His presence. This is the hope that believers can have without fear of contradiction. Heaven, however, is not the permanent home of believers, but is simply a holding place until after the final judgment when a new heaven and a new earth will be created.[70]

---

[68]   Luke 20:38

[69]   2 Cor. 5:8

[70]   Rev. 21:1

Hell

The bible is clear that hell is a place of eternal punishment and torment.[71] It is a place that exists outside of time or rather, in eternity. It was made originally for the devil and his angels, but unrepentant, sinful men will go there as well.[72]

Luke 12:5 shows that God has the authority to put men there, but the bible does not clearly show why some unbelievers are condemned to hell as soon as they die, while others continue to exist in the earth realm.

Many believe that hell is metaphorical or allegorical. The bible does not support this view, as Jesus made references to its existence more than once.

The final judgment has not taken place yet, but once the final sentence has been passed, unrepentant men will share the same fate as the devil and his fallen angels.

Earth realm

We have already established that human spirits can continue to function in the earth realm. They are called ghosts or disembodied spirits. Every culture on planet earth presently has or has had anecdotal reports or experiences with ghosts. As just stated, we are unsure and the bible is not clear as to why some are immediately condemned to hell (as was the rich man in the story of Lazarus) and some are allowed to continue to harass others the earth realm, but the fact that they do is clear. It may simply be, in

---

71   Matt. 9:43, Luke 16:23

72   Matt. 25:41

part, that the will to move on to the next realm is lacking in the spirits that decide to stay on the earth. It may also be that many are so attached to the things of the world that it is hard for them to release it; for where your treasure is there you heart will be![73]

Once a person has died and shed the body, their right to continue to function in the earth realm has been taken away. Remember, it is the body that legitimizes actions in the earth. Contact or cooperation with these spirits is forbidden by God, since their time in the earth is finished and they are in an in-between state awaiting judgment. To conjure them with Ouija boards or by other means, converse with them or cooperate with them, is to allow them to re-introduce their particular slant on evil in the world.

These spirits are most effective when they can gain access to a human body. They do this by getting the person they desire to inhabit to agree with thoughts, feelings or ideas and desires as presented to the mind or emotions. Whenever one witnesses a radical change of personality or habits in another person, it is evidence of the influence of another personality or spirit.

Hollywood movies, a desire for pleasure, drugs and liberal philosophies that encourage people to do what they **feel**, have opened the flood gates for spirits to gain even greater access to the population at even younger ages than in times past. This is compounded by social media, social pressure to conform to particular views and political correctness. Understand too that wickedness and perversion *must* increase in the days ahead, since people in the world have not learnt how to stand against the

---

[73]   Matt 6:21

spiritual influences that have created this deluge of *self* gratification and perversion.[74]

As more angry, vengeful, lustful, avaricious, perverted and murderous people die, so will we have more of them in the earth realm in a disembodied state looking for bodies to continue to live out their desires through. I also believe that the present crest of social acceptance that sexual perversion enjoys today is directly related to the large numbers of people who died from promiscuous lifestyles and AIDS in the 1980's and 1990's and the influences of their spirits on popular culture.

Paradise

While he was hanging on the cross, nailed between two thieves, one of them confessed faith in Jesus. The Lord said to him, "today you will be with me in paradise."[75] Jesus could have easily used the word heaven, but He intentionally did not.

In Luke 16:19-31, we read a most interesting account given by the Lord Jesus. He recounts the story of a wealthy man and a poor beggar. The wealthy man died and descended into flames (hell) and was tormented. The poor man later died and was carried by angels to a place called Abrahams bosom (notice the Lord did not say heaven). The rich man, tormented in the flames, had full recollection of his life and status while on earth and also had awareness of various sensations and desires. He could feel the heat of the flames and thirst. He knew the poor man by name and

---

[74]   2 Tim. 3:1-5 KJV

[75]   Luke 23:43

desired for that man to do for him what he had not done for the poor man in his own lifetime. The story also tells us that there is a gulf fixed that does not allow those in either place to travel out of it. The righteous dead cannot go down to Hades (hell) and the wicked cannot come up.

Prior to Jesus' death and resurrection, paradise was the place where those God had declared righteous would go after death. However, because their spirits are not regenerated, they do not enter the same "heaven" that those with regenerated spirits do. This helps us to better understand the passage in 1 Peter 3:18, 19, which tells us about Jesus preaching to spirits confined in a holding place after His death. This is also the place where those who have never heard the gospel, but are righteous by the standards of God's law, go when they die.[76] The bible says that although they do not have the law they are a law unto themselves, because the law of God is written in the conscience of *all* men. Men can choose to violate their own consciences! Since God is just, He would not condemn to hell those who have never heard the gospel. However, those who have not heard the gospel and live morally impure lives have been seduced by unclean spirits and have violated the law of God which in the *conscience* of man.

Additionally, in 2 Corinthians 12:2-4, Paul tells us that he visited paradise during a spiritual experience, but he called it the third heaven; a place that is distinct from where the throne of God is.

---

[76]   Rom. 2:14

CHAPTER SEVEN

A City Without Walls

Whoever has no rule over his own spirit is like a city broken-down without walls (Prov. 25:28 NJKV).

As he thinks in his heart so is he (Prov. 23:7).

In ancient times walls were the primary means of defense for a city. Once people started to congregate in large groups, protection from marauders and invading armies became essential. The walls had to be both tall and wide enough to withstand the assaults of the enemy. Failure to construct a wall that fully enclosed the community or city would prove disastrous. The wall would also be the point from which defending armies would oppose the advances of the foreign army. The weakest point in the city wall is where the enemy would focus his attention.

The scripture here is telling us that mans spirit is the *individuals* responsibility and that knowing how to rule over or control one's spirit is essential to maintaining *self* control i.e. control of one's self. When a person either fails to control or loses control of their spirit, then the enemy can come in and control that person. This is interesting, simply because it is teaching us that even unbelievers can resist the enemy if they learn how to control their own spirit. This is one of the key reasons for clearly defining boundaries and instilling discipline in children.

Therefore, walls are representative of the values and standards at the level of a community or nation. It provides general protection for all, but the city wall did not exempt the individual from establishing his own walls of personal protection for his house. It was Gods intention that His laws would provide the general defense for the community and then each individual would reinforce those truths in his own person and for his own house. This is why, undisciplined children who do not have clearly defined boundaries become adults without the same. And as a result, we are seeing more and more children and adults, being allowed to embrace ideas that completely distort their fundamental identities, in the face of established science and commonsense!

Controlling ones spirit, however, is not the same as being born again; it simply means that a person knows who they are as an individual and chooses whether they want to do something or not. They are in control of themselves and as a result, they have the capacity to exercise more restraint to the urges, impulses and temptations that may arise within them. Conversely a person lacking in self control can be spiritually alive, but morally compromised. In the believer, the goal is to be both spiritually alive and morally upright, remembering that our basis for morality should be on the basis of God's word and not worldly values, which are constantly shifting.

The wall, as already alluded to, is developed in part, by parental upbringing and discipline or correction. It is the responsibility of parents to guide their children in the right ways of God's moral laws and to correct their behavior using appropriate means. It is essential for a strong association to be created in the mind of the child between disobedience of moral laws and punishment. Since a failure to discipline children for breaking God's moral laws will inevitably result in them being subject to the consequences of temporal civil law (prison) or natural law (unwanted pregnancies, sexually transmitted diseases etc.) and eternal separation from God. Actions do have consequences. This is also an explanation for why there are higher levels of crime, violence and poverty in communities where there is a lack of proper parental supervision and discipline. They are environments in which evil flourishes because of a lack of self control!

The obvious decline in learning, and understanding the importance of God's laws has created a permissive society with variable moral standards. This has created a lack of uniformity in the values expressed by society at large. It has also seen the boundaries of morality pushed further and further away from biblical standards. In the past women were prized for their chastity, now they are lauded in mainstream media for dispensing with it, often repeatedly, and those who want to preserve some modicum of decency are ridiculed. It has become far more important to have a curated *image* than to have actual *character*. Integrity, honesty and loyalty are virtually bywords, all because of the departure society has made from God's moral law. They have become qualities that people expect from others, but have no desire to cultivate in their own lives.

All disobedience to God's moral or spiritual laws creates a point of weakness in the wall protecting a person's spirit. Persons who may not have had the appropriate instruction as children have virtually no defense to the incursions of the enemy. Once a person loses control of their spirit, they are spiritually compromised and the enemy will enter. It is this loss of spiritual control that drives young people to experiment, and that experimentation causes even more erosion of the remaining walls. It is important to understand that once the wall has been breached and adequate control gained, only the enemy has a right to control what enters, how much enters and the purpose they will attempt to fulfill through the person now in their control. The person will now be filled with thoughts, feelings and desires that they will act upon. He now becomes whatever is going on in his heart, because a man *is* what he thinks *in his heart*; the inner man.[77]

The current onslaught the world faces with same sex relationships and those who address themselves as 'transgender' individuals is evidence of this principle. There are those who opine that they always had same sex attractions or 'know' they were the opposite sex, they are lying. They say that from they were children they knew they were different. The truth is that they may have had thoughts, feelings or desires based on the spirits influencing them, but it was *their* internalizing and believing the lies they were told and then acting upon those lies that made

---

[77]   Prov. 23:7

them what they claim to be. This is a spiritual law and it matters not who violates it. Are children not subject to the laws of gravity in spite of their ignorance? As in the natural, so too in the spirit! This is why proper parenting is so important.

Consider that no one is born a thief and that no person who is called a thief is called one because he *struggles* with the desire to steal. It is his *acting* on that desire that makes him a thief and creates an even stronger desire to steal again, until it becomes habitual and in some cases uncontrollable. It is his acting on the desire to take something that is not his that makes him a thief. Thought, desire and action cause a man to become a thing; anything. This is true of all things, good or evil.

Consider how a man becomes a liar, humanitarian, philanthropist, rapist or murderer; it all starts with the thought and then a growing desire and a corresponding action. This is also true of the behaviors the world calls addictions. An addiction, as discussed in an earlier chapter, is simply a state where the spirit of the person is no longer in control and instead they are in bondage to or controlled by another spirit(s). The controlling spirit is in charge of the city as it were and makes the person commit many acts they may not want to. Being in this state creates torment. All addicts are tormented and can readily recognize that there is another person(s) in them, driving them to do undesirable things. All addicts will tell you that when they first started to do whatever the activity was, it was fun, but once the spirit became entrenched, they were in torment.

There are many socially acceptable ways of losing control of self, and people generally like the feeling of being less inhibited; less in control. Lowered inhibitions however, tend to make individuals more suggestible and serve as a gateway for inappropriate relationships or use of other drugs. The addictive potential of a drug serves as an indicator of the strength of the spirit attached with the drug. This is the reason that cocaine or heroin is more addictive than marijuana or alcohol, but all mind altering drugs break down the walls of self control and create the opportunity for the entrance of unclean spirits. It is not in each and every instance that a person loses self control that they will be immediately be entered by an unclean spirit, but the risk increases significantly with the frequency of losing control. I am even skeptical of legal drugs like ketamine, a *dissociative* anesthetic which produces hallucinations and a state of *detachment* in its subjects, as any detached person is not in control of themselves and is at risk of the conditions described above.

Another area that cannot be minimized is the ability of the enemy to use pain as a way to gain access to a subject. Pain is a ubiquitous part of the human experience, but when people suffer intense emotional or physical pain, they become very vulnerable to the suggestions (lies) of the enemy. If he can convince a person that they are not loved, not smart, not appreciated, not good enough, not valued, accepted etc., then he can encourage them to retreat into themselves, i.e. become more *self* absorbed. When a person internalizes and becomes absorbed with self, they become encased within themselves and are cut off from others and God physically, emotionally and spiritually. The lies they believe become *their* truth, a deep well from which extrication is near impossible. They lose the ability to control themselves (thoughts, actions, moods etc) and become controlled, by their false thoughts and feelings!

Self control is a word that has progressively negative connotations when it comes to the ideology called "self expression". In truth, how can you truly express yourself if you do not know who you are, and how can you know who you are, if you do not know the One who made you and why He made you? What you find then is that most people are, in truth, expressing the idea of who they *think* they are, based on thoughts that have not originated from themselves! Body piercings, tattoos, and other outward expressions, serve as the canvas for most of today's efforts for the young, and not so young, to exhibit who they think they are, their individuality. But doesn't one's DNA or fingerprint do that already? In truth, you are more than a tattoo; who you are cannot be reduced to body art, how you express yourself sexually or any such thing. It is a little more complicated than that.

Therefore, we reiterate that *any* violation of God's laws or anything that causes a person to lose control of self, serves as a portal of entry for unclean spirits. We have already shown that these come primarily in the form of thoughts. But how much easier it is to control a person's thoughts if their emotions are vigorously stirred with pride, greed, anger, hurt, lust, rejection, offence and the list goes on and on. The presence of these feelings unleashes a torrent of thoughts in the mind of a person. Do you really believe all of those thoughts rushing through your mind or sudden urges of anger originate with you?

Consider the advice of Psalm 1:1, it says that the man who does not walk in the counsel, advice or suggestions of an ungodly person is blessed. We often associate this passage with "real" people, the flesh and blood kind, but what about people who are unseen? When a person is angry, offended, rejected and suddenly have other negative emotions, if honest, they will admit that there are actual conversations that occur in their head; a multiplicity of thoughts, suggestions and plans that form to encourage them to address their grievances or to pursue a desired end result. Negative, offended angry spirits are attracted to the negative energy that emanates from a person who is hurting. The more a person listens to the voices of these spirits and act out their advice, the more they become akin to the spirits who are advising them. The more they become controlled by those spirits. This is why emotional instability is so dangerous; it makes it easy for people to be controlled by a whole host of different spirits. It also explains why it is impossible to have a rational discussion between parties where one side presents facts and the other counters with outrage and or violence. It is also why pleasure or a feeling of power is always associated with strong emotional occurrences. The urge, impulse, feeling or desire creates a Pavlovian stimulus response cycle that is very difficult to break, even when the consequences of yielding to the illogical desires destroy a person's life.

Pavlov showed that if you ring a bell and then give a dog a treat several times, you can eventually encourage the dog to salivate simply by ringing the bell. As a result, a certain stimulus can create a specific pre-conditioned response. This tactic, properly applied, encourages people under the worlds system of government to live their lives based on what they *think or feel* when exposed to certain stimuli. The devil always offers pleasure as the reward for disobeying God's law, but the good feeling never lasts as long as the consequences.

Movies particularly with horror, graphic violence and sexual content are another point of entry. The bible teaches that the eyes are the lamp of the body or the soul through which light or darkness can enter.[78] The eyes are a direct point of entrance into mans spirit.

In summary, God created man firstly to have control of himself and then control of his environment. When we fail at controlling ourselves, we have created the prerequisite for being controlled.

---

[78] Matt. 6:22-23

CHAPTER EIGHT

Transfer of Spirits

... put on different garments so they will not transfer holiness to the people through their garments. Eze. 44:19

Now that we have already tackled many controversial areas and challenged many established belief systems, why stop now! Let's continue headfirst into this next topic.

I want to begin by establishing the importance of understanding spiritual laws, which are principles established by God for the way something operate in the spirit realm. We understand that man was created to have relationship and fellowship with God *in* his spirit. Hopefully, we have established that perversion of that law has allowed other spirits to access and control man instead. We have also discussed that a man will be controlled by the spirit that he yields to. These are spiritual laws. But it is also a law that the spirit in a man can be transferred to people or objects.

The ability for spirits to be transferred between people or objects is extremely misunderstood. One of the clearest examples of a spiritual transfer is found in Numbers 11: 16-17, where God takes *some* of the spirit in Moses and places it upon 70 elders so that they could give him aid in administrative activities.

In the Old Testament, God speaks of defilement or the polluting of people, places and things and routinely orders the destruction of the defiled or unclean things. The question is why destroy something because it is defiled? What is it that makes the person or thing defiled? We can review the Greek meaning of several words translated as defiled:

- Strongs H2930- (tame') to become morally impure or unclean. To be polluted.
- Strongs H2490- (chalal)- to violate the honor of, to pollute, to break one's word.
- Strongs H1351- (ga'al) to pollute, desecrate
- Strongs G2840- (koinoo) to make ceremonially unclean, profane
- Strongs G5351- (phtheiro) to corrupt, to destroy, to deprave
- Strongs G733- (arsenokites) one who lies with a male as with a female, a sodomite
- Strongs G3392- (miaino) to stain with sin, to contaminate.

In all of these definitions one thing is clear, the one who is defiled has been polluted, contaminated or has become depraved through contact with something or someone the Lord commanded no contact with. Since man is a spirit and man can become polluted, the act of becoming impure or unclean cannot be making reference to man's body solely, but rather his spirit. The only thing that can defile a spirit is another spirit.

The simple explanation is that a spirit is associated with the forbidden activities and the appropriate remedy had to be applied. In the case of the nation of Israel the remedy was a sin offering of some kind or death, depending on the offence. Many do not understand that violation of spiritual law has spiritual consequences that are independent of the atoning work of Christ's death.

It is very important to understand that the primary means through which the devil usurped control of the world, was because of his understanding of spiritual laws. This understanding gives him a remarkable advantage over those who are ignorant of such laws. One way we can understand and increase our knowledge of spiritual laws is to simply pay attention to two things: what God commands us to *do* or *not do* (this shows us the positive and negative attributes of the law) **and** what the devil does (which is always a twisting of the law). The purpose of God's laws, instructions or advice is to protect us from the consequences of breaking a spiritual law and to restrict or hinder the access the devil has to our lives; because the devil *wants* us to break the laws and so give him greater access to our lives. We can be sure that whenever there is a local or global trend that increases in popularity there is a spiritual law being transgressed and the devil is gaining greater control in the lives of the deceived. Almost all socially accepted behavior violates the laws of God. The devil created nothing; he simply manipulates or perverts the truth. So once we see the truth applied, we can be sure the opposite would gain prominence in his domain.

One aspect of spiritual law that we want to consider is the concept of being able to transfer spirits. This means that a spirit or spirits that one person has can be imparted to another person(s) or things, causing the influence of that spirit to be manifest in the other person, or causing the spirit in a thing (object) to influence others. Let us consider the example of laying on of hands, one example of which is of Moses **transferring the spirit of wisdom to Joshua in Deut. 34:9.**

The word lay (Strongs H7971 shalach) means to send out or to send forth.

(Strongs G2007- epitithemi) means to impose upon in a friendly or hostile way, to attack one.

(Strongs G1911- epiballo) to put on, to rush in

By looking at the definitions noted above, we can see that when a person lays hands on another person or thing, they are able, through an act of their will, to send forth something from themselves to that person or thing. It also seems to suggest that the impartation or transfer is intentional, deliberate and under the control of the one laying on the hands. The practice of the laying on of hands to transmit a blessing or a calling is prevalent through the Old Testament.[79]

---

[79]   Gen. 48:14, Num. 27:23

The priest would lay his hands on an animal to transfer the sins of the people to the animal.[80]

Acts 8:17, 19:6, clearly showed that the Holy Spirit can be transferred through the laying on of hands.

Jesus and the disciples healed by the laying on of hands.[81]

In relation to inanimate objects, Acts 19:12 showed that even Paul's handkerchiefs and aprons were taken to the sick and evil spirits left them. And the scripture referenced at the beginning of this chapter showed a quality like holiness, could be transferred to garments and then to others.

One of the principles that we have already observed is that God expects man to exhibit control in all areas where man has been given authority, whereas evil spirits are forceful and imposing. The spirit of a prophet is to be under the control of the prophet, is one passage that shows the level of control men are to have over their spirits.[82]

In another passage, Jesus was giving His disciples instructions prior to sending them out to preach and made a very interesting statement, advising them that if they stayed in a house where they were well treated, then they could have *their peace* rest upon the house, **but** they could also have their peace *return* to them if they were not treated well.[83] Imagine that one aspect of something they possessed spiritually could be isolated and allowed to pervade the space that they were in by their choice. This passage in particular

---

[80] Exo. 29:15, Lev. 8:14, 16:21, Num. 8:12

[81] Mark 5:23, 16:18, Luke 4:40, 13:13, Acts 28:8

[82] 1 Cor. 14:32

[83] Matt. 10: 12-13

causes me to think of the dark, heavy, oppressive, 'creepy' or light, peaceful feelings that may be experienced upon walking into certain places. There is no scientific explanation for the awareness of these varying states of being that a person can sense in their environment, but these passages help us to understand that there are many dimensions in the spirit realm that we simply do not understand and that we should not ignore.

In each instance when hands were laid upon a person it was voluntary and the person was open, or expecting to receive something during the impartation. The principle then is that healing, blessings and the Holy Spirit can be transferred from one person to another. As this is a spiritual principle, then sickness, curses and unclean spirits can also be transferred. During the process of transference, the spirit is not diminished. In other words the "amount" of the Holy Spirit in existence in the transferor, for example, is not reduced by impartation to another person.

Leviticus 5: 2-5 makes it clear that a person can become unclean by touching certain items or even making certain decisions to acts against another person. This means that touch provides a medium through which a person becomes unclean or defiled.

Leviticus 18 gives an extensive list of sins that could not only cause the offender to become defiled, but the land they were in as well. Other passages that make reference to this are:

- Contact with or seeking out mediums or spirits caused defilement through association- Leviticus. 19:31.

- Touching anything belonging to defiled people causes defilement- Numbers. 16:26, Numbers 19:22.
- Defilement through sexual activity- Leviticus. 18, Numbers 25:1.
- Idols defile- Deuteronomy. 7:25.
- Do not bring a morally impure thing into your house- Deuteronomy 7:26

There are also passages that refer to defilement of God's temple.[84] If the Old Testament temple, the place God had a dwelling place, could be defiled, then it stands to reason that as believers who are God's temple, so can we be!

---

[84] 2 Chr 29:5, 16, Eze. 5:11, 23:38, 44:7

CHAPTER NINE

Doctrines of Devils

The Holy Spirit tell us clearly that in the last times some will turn away from the true faith; they will follow deceptive spirits and teachings that come from demons (1 Tim. 4:1 NLT).

They will say it is wrong to be married and wrong to eat certain foods .... (1 Tim. 4:3 NLT)

The two passages above reveal something of tremendous importance, namely that demons can and do teach. We have touched on this idea briefly already, but let's explore the cultural nuances of these statements a bit more closely.

In order to teach anything, one must have those who are willing to listen and apply what is being taught. It is in the fertile soil of confusion during the human experience and man's separation from God, that seeds, ideas and desires are sown. The confusion and frustration that is characteristic of this earthly experience is the result of us having lost our "God connection" or the ability to be regulated or inspired from above. In this condition, persons no longer know what *normal* is; they become susceptible to being seduced, deceived and then used as agents to propagate specific ideas.

Let us consider the word inspire. All "great" ideas to produce music, books, art, movies, religion, technology and philosophy etc., were *inspired* were they not? Inspire means to fill someone with the urge or ability to *do* or *feel* something, usually creative, but we know that people can also be inspired to be violent, hateful, scheming and so forth. The question is where does this inspiration come from?

Very often those who are inspired are minding their own business when a thought, feeling, urge or impulse arises within them. It is when they *yield* to the influence (accept, engage with and ponder) that the thoughts or feelings develop into something more tangible. It is as though a door or window has opened up in their mind and they are able to see something they did not see or understand before. *They may not be able to articulate it at first, but they 'know' something that they did not know before.* This is the creative process briefly explained. As the inspiration is developed, it forms parameters within which it will function and the recipient of that inspiration, once thoroughly convinced, will begin to share their idea or create the concept previously only seen in their mind. This is the faith principle at work.

We have already shown that spirits can teach by thoughts, urges and impulses to motivate a person to do certain things, but they can also appear in dreams and visions and can introduce ideas to shape and influence human ideology and behavior. Consider for instance that there is only one name that is universally blasphemed or used to utter profanities, and it's not Buddha, Allah or Confucius.

The list below is not intended to be, nor can it be exhaustive, but in light of what has been discussed so far, is to encourage some thought about the areas presented and is not intended to offend.

Philosophy

There is nothing more powerful or destructive than an idea. Ideas usually outlive their progenitors. With ideas, the world as we know it was shaped and continues to devolve; some might say, evolve.

Ideas shape and influence our systems of thought, economics, religion, etc. As individuals, we are a repository of beliefs and values, fashioned in the image of men and women we have never met. Through the millennia certain beliefs, philosophies and ideologies persist. Just think of Aristotle, Socrates, Kant, Marx, Nietzsche and others and you are able to associate certain systems of thought with each person. The list of people who have influenced present belief is too large to comprehend, but where did all of these different ideas, philosophies and perspectives originate?

The great power of philosophy is that at some level, visceral or intellectual, it seems to resonate with certain aspects of the human experience, making it "true" to the person having that particular experience. It greatest limitation however, is that the fallible mind is the vehicle through which attempts are made to explain various aspects of our existence. Although logic is an excellent tool for arriving at conclusions, it has an inherent problem; the initial premise must be correct in order to come to the correct logical conclusion. If one started to button a shirt at the wrong hole, each button will fit into the next hole nicely until you arrive at the last button. That's the fundamental problem with using logic solely as a tool to arrive at truth. Though not completely useless as an approach to understanding the world and its problems, the mind cannot process a variable it has not considered or a concept it cannot grasp. There are many things which lie beyond our ability to understand.

Although there have been some Christian philosophers, to a large degree philosophy has been secular and, in my opinion, has only served to muddy the waters of human existence by introducing concepts designed to create the illusion of opening our minds or broadening our perspectives, all the while turning our eyes from the God who made us, to others, ourselves or to nature. The man standing on the 50th floor of a skyscraper has a completely different perspective than a man on ground level. Philosophy metaphorically, tries to get the person on ground level to see what the person on the 50th floor of the skyscraper sees, which is still only a partial view of reality. In my view, after religion, philosophy has been one of the greatest weapons the devil has used to deceive and enslave mankind.

Consider this one example for instance. We would readily acknowledge that in spite of the many advances that have been made in science and technology, there is so much more that is still unknown about the world around us. In fact, it seems that the more we learn, the more we realize how much more there is to learn, and this is one of the reasons why I am often intrigued and befuddled by atheists. There is no one on the earth, including experts in any field that knows 100% of all possible information about that particular subject. What doctor knows 100% of all there is to know in or about medicine, or a physicist about physics or musician about music? If experts only know a part of all there is to know about subjects of their specialty, then how much can one truly know about all other matters? This must mean that there are truths or knowledge that exists outside of their current points of reference or knowledge! Only God knows 100% of all there is to know and that is why He alone can be trusted and it is also why He is the only source of ultimate truth!

The Bible calls him a fool who makes an emphatic statement that there is no God.[85] The reason the bible can make this bold statement is obvious. One would have to know all there is to know about *everything* in order to say with certainty that God does not exist. If there is even the remotest possibility that the person saying "there is no God", does not know something, then how can he know everything? That uncertainty then declares their folly when they attempt to speak authoritatively. In other words one must know all there is to know about a thing to authoritatively state that something in relation to that thing is or is not so, otherwise it is merely an opinion. Therefore, the various arguments that are used to support atheistic philosophy, while seemingly cogent, are pseudo intellectual at best and are very often hinged on the failure to understand the nature of God, the nature of man and how the God of the bible works in human affairs.

---

[85]   Psalm 14:1

When you combine the 'shortcomings' of *religion* with misunderstandings regarding the nature and person of God, there will be the reinforcing of the 'truth' of the non-existence of God in the atheists mind. This 'truth' becomes self-delusion, since it is impossible to objectively disprove the existence of God. The foundations of atheism therefore are presumption, arrogance and pride, not a search for truth. But look at how many people use their bodies and its abilities to write and preach this illogical idea and how many more imbibe it!

Religion

To date, I have yet to come across a culture that has not had various forms of religious expression or rituals and those required to perform them. Every ancient culture had those persons who claimed the power to, or who were entrusted with the task of 'appealing' to a higher power, i.e., contacting the spirit world. This very fact is evidence of a longing in man for re-connection with his spiritual Father. Through religion, the devil offers a myriad of choices for how this 'reconnection' should occur. One of the most jarring things many will come to learn is that God is not a member of their denomination or system of worship, for He stands far above all of that.

Demons are behind the influences of **all** religious thought and were/are the teachers of **all** *religious* leaders. They simply need a person to propagate their ideas. The recipient of these beliefs is usually titled (shaman, priest, bishop and so forth). That person(s) is the bridge by which spoken or written spiritual ideas travel to the masses. These demons encourage the worship, promotion or elevation of anything that is not the one, true God. Notice that the Greek definitions of demons we reviewed earlier revolve primarily around the idea of gods (little 'g') and worship.

It has wrongly been said, especially by prominent atheists, that religions are man-made, that is incorrect; they are demonically inspired. In the hands of demons, religions serve a three-fold purpose:

1. To take worship from God and draw it to themselves;
2. To offer a 'spiritual buffet'- increase the fare of religious choices, creating confusion and making it more difficult to get to know the God of the bible;
3. To capitalize on spiritual hunger. But because religion is unable to satisfy the spiritual cravings of man the devil wants to magnify the emptiness and frustration one feels, causing them to give up on God and religion all together.

Around religious ideas, rituals are constructed to create standards by which a person can 'connect' to god and judge how 'good' or 'bad' they are. Once you combine religious ideology and ritual, you have a powerful combination.

We must appreciate that religion, in truth, is as old as man himself and being a priest, or conjurer are among the oldest professions and often strikingly similar to the oldest. Worship is an effort to express externally the innate desire man has to acknowledge the existence of a supreme being, using rituals and an ethos to shape or guide moral conduct. The bible teaches that man was designed to worship and if he does not worship the One true God, he **will** worship lesser gods (demons) or himself.

Consider the lengths many cultures went to in order to appease the gods they served including human sacrifice. At some point human sacrifice was practiced in some form in many Asian, European, African and Central and South American countries. In spite of the fact that this practice was forbidden in ancient Israel, wayward kings often followed the religious traditions of heathen nations as shown by offering sacrifices to demons, which are not God, to gods they had not known before. To "gods only *recently arrived…*,"[86] and sacrificing their sons and daughters to devils.[87] Paul states plainly in 1 Corinthians 10:20 that the sacrifices of pagans are offered to demons, not to God.

Earlier, it was stated that *all* religions are demonically inspired and we have also stated more than once, that Jesus Christ did not come to earth to establish a religion, but to allow man to be spiritually reconnected *relationally* with his Maker. Christianity initially was not perceived to be a religion by its adherents, but was a derogatory label used to identify those in relationship with Jesus Christ. It was a death sentence. Today that has changed and a person can be labeled a Christian if he or she is born into a family that is actively or nominally involved in 'the church'. Christianity as a religion can also accept, tolerate and ordinate 'gay or transgender' clergy and a whole host of other things, but the Kingdom of God, which is based on **relationship** with God, recognizes no such thing. The very idea that one can claim they are Christian and actively practice lifestyles that the bible declares sinful is an example of this. They might say, the bible says "…

---

[86]   Deu. 32:17 NLT

[87]   Psalms 106:37

to love" and "… it is wrong to judge others" are examples of statements devilishly misused to paint the offenders of Gods laws as victims of bigotry and those who seek to uphold those laws as villains. They have not pondered several things: firstly, why would God send His only begotten Son to die to *free* us from the power of sin, if it was His desire that we do not repent of it, but rather celebrate and wallow in it, like a pig in the mud? Secondly, how is a person "judging" if they merely restate what the bible has already made a judgment on? Lastly, many do not realize that men can make any law they want using civil procedures, but what is "right" by civil law can still violate God's moral law. They are not the same thing.

It is my view, that where the objective is the propagation of denominational beliefs or a refashioning of the church to look like the world and not the cultivation of a personal relationship with God through Jesus by the Holy Spirit, then it is demonically inspired. This is simply because the efforts that are made will not bring a person closer to the God they are seeking. It bears repeating, that Jesus taught emphatically that God hates religion and Jesus Himself did not come to earth to establish a religion called Christianity, but to encourage man to recognize that something is missing from his life. That missing thing is a relationship with the God who created him. A relationship can be initiated by trusting in God to save him from his disconnected state, simply by believing that Jesus came to reconnect the relationship.[88]

Historically, religion has been a scourge to the earth. It has and continues to motivate many wars, injustices and atrocities in its

---

[88] John 3:16

name and has caused many to question the justice and sovereignty of a God who would allow these things to happen. Many have abandoned all forms of religion; they believe, and tout themselves as atheists (this idea has been discussed earlier). They have created atheistic states and philosophies to express their displeasure at the abuses of religion. They have changed nothing. Their praise and adoration is simply given over to social, educational or intellectual pursuits and time will prove that these continuing social experiments will yield the same fruit as communism and socialism has – frustration, despair and emptiness.

Ancient civilizations with their temple priests, shrine prostitutes, human sacrifice and loyal devotees all had one thing in common- a god or gods that could not be satiated. There was always more that the gods wanted; they always demanded more. And often in the process, humans were encouraged to debase themselves from their intended dignity as the apex of God's creation, to do that which God deemed vile. There has to be some perverse pleasure demons get out of watching man live so far below their God intended purpose.

Occultism

Since man is a spiritual being, he has always been aware of the supernatural, but has not always been able to understand it. This lack of understanding creates curiosity and the desire to want to explore that world. Ignorant of the dangers and punishments associated with tampering with the spirit world, the devil was able to take advantage of mans ignorant curiosity and entice some people to explore it. Witches, wizards, witchcraft and necromancy are all real, though not as Hollywood portrays.

We have determined that demons can teach, but how can they be trusted to teach us about themselves and how the unseen world works? The answer is that they cannot be trusted at all, which is why God forbids contact with them. Note that God would not forbid contact with them, unless contact could be made with them! In many places the scriptures warn that man should not practice saying spells or fortunetelling e.g. Leviticus 19:26.

The bible is clear, that the study and practice of magic and seeking knowledge of the occult is forbidden. The admonition not to indulge or explore this hidden world has been ignored by many over the millennia. The knowledge, power and influence derived from the occult are real, but it is also dangerous.

Remember the principle way that people are influenced is by the introduction of ideas associated with feelings (inspiration) and subsequently yielding to those ideas.

In Exodus 7: 8-12, the bible recounts the story of Moses and his brother Aaron going to pharaoh to request the release of the nation of Israel from Egyptian bondage. Aaron was commanded by God to throw down his staff (a tall walking stick) and it became a snake. Pharaoh, unfazed by this display, called some of his magicians and sorcerers who also did the exact same thing. We are not talking about the sleight of hand or illusions that many 'magicians' indulge in today; rather we are witnessing the physical transformation of one object into another, seemingly at the behest of men. In several instances, pharaoh's magicians were able to replicate the miracles of Moses. They were able to turn water into blood, conjure lice and frogs etc. This story shows us several things, firstly that it is possible to have supernatural power from a source other than God.

Secondly, the power of darkness is real and seemingly can be controlled by man, but thirdly and most importantly that the power of God is greater than all the power of the devil; for Aaron's staff ate all the staffs of the magicians and none of them were able to undo the plagues which God had caused.

Consider though how those magicians might have gotten to the point where they could flagrantly display in public that which they practiced in darkness, being taught by their demonic teachers. Consider too what price was paid or sacrifices they may have made to acquire those abilities. This is the appeal of the occult, power over others and the environment. Deep meditation, astral projection, use of spirit guides, sending curses and all other manners of consorting with demons is real, dangerous and forbidden by God. This also highlights the reason why people should not be moved by or actively pursue 'supernatural' signs and wonders, for what is more important is the *source* of them!

This present day fascination with the occult has seen a stream of television programs, movies etc glamorizing the occult and sensationalizing its allure. In fact, social media, television, movies and music are now the primary tools used for mass propagation and promulgation of occult and demonic ideas. It no longer takes generations to change a society's perspectives, now it can take days.

Reincarnation

There are many religions that have as a basic tenet that the soul persists after death being reborn in another bodily form, sometimes a lower form as a animal, sometimes a 'higher' form. Different religions have different ideas about how this happens. The bible teaches that man dies *once*, after that he waits to be judged.[89] Resurgence in a belief in reincarnation has been fostered by various aspects of Eastern religions gaining popularity in the West and the growth of what has been called the New Age movement. We must recognize the popular appeal reincarnation can have. Who wants to believe that after this life is done you now wait to be judged for what you did in your body while on earth? Nobody wants to be judged; that proposition is the hedonist's nightmare.

There have been many new age proponents and authors who have written that they have had experiences of their past lives. I have found that in 99% of the past life stories I have heard, the person was always affluent and powerful. That alone should raise questions, but the most striking story relating to reincarnation is that of the Dalai Lama. He is purportedly the incarnation (the enlightened being) of compassion.

The current Dalai Lama is the 14th such incarnation. At the time of the death of the Dalai Lama a search is started in Tibet for the new incarnation. This is a process that can sometime take several years. The person or persons selected, usually a child, is chosen if they are able to identify specific personal items owned by

---

[89]   Heb. 9:27

the recently deceased Dalai Lama, along with other predetermined criteria. When multiple persons are identified, there are additional criteria for selection. Here we see a culture that has emerged in which people are ready to allow their bodies to be vessels that the spirits of the deceased can re-enter for the purpose of continuing to exert their influence in this realm. Does this really support re-incarnation, especially since the new candidate may have already been alive when the Dalai Lama died? It does however support the idea of re-entry of a human spirit into a different body.

If we consider what we have learnt thus far, we know that deceased spirits can enter the body of the living, we also know that they have memories of their past life. Is it reasonable to argue then that the occurrences of the phenomenon of so called past life experiences are simply deceased human spirits, relaying events as they experienced them or are demons deceiving the person having the experience? In any event reincarnation is not an idea supported by the bible.

Prayers to the dead

The Catholic Church is pre-eminent among Western religions for having a system that promotes prayers to the dead. The most prominent dead person in Catholicism that is a recipient of prayer is Mary, Jesus' mother. She has also been credited with visions, healings and a whole host of other supernatural occurrences throughout the history of the Catholic Church. The Catholic Church has also not discouraged prayer to a cadre of other 'esteemed' Catholics it terms saints, forgetting that the bible strictly forbids attempts to communicate with or to pray to the dead[90], i.e. those who have died but are existing in another plane. Not one instance of Old or New Testament prayer was directed to those who would qualify as saints, those who had died or the mother of Jesus. This practice of Mary worship was developed several centuries after Jesus' death. Prayers are to be directed to God *alone*, for who else has the power to hear and answer? Also the bible teaches clearly that there is only **one** mediator between God and man, Jesus Himself.[91]

Abstaining from Meats

There are a variety of religious groups that abstain from meats for a variety of reasons. The bible teaches in the introductory passage above, that the teaching that it is wrong to eat meat is a demon-inspired doctrine. I can only imagine this also applies to plant based "meats" as well. For an individual to abstain from meat for a health or personal reason is one thing, but for a group to teach that it is wrong, is another. For everything God created is good and *nothing* is to be rejected if it is received with thanksgiving[92]. Additionally, a person ought not to feel pressured to eat or not to eat meat because of the judgments of others.[93]

There are those who have argued that the original diet of man was fruit and vegetables based on Gods instructions to Adam. They forget that Adam fell, the earth was cursed and God gave new instructions to Noah after the flood that he could eat

---

[90]   Deut 18:11

[91]   1Tim. 2:5

[92]   1 Tim. 4:4

[93]   Col. 2:16

everything *except* the blood of animals.[94] Later the list of animals was restricted in laws given to Moses. Paul continues the same thought as shown above. The bible basically teaches that whether or not you should eat certain meats is really a matter of your personal choice or conscience.[95]

Forbidding to Marry

The Catholic Church has been in the news for many years now because of repeated scandals related to sexual misconduct, primarily by its priests. There are also those priests who have been defrocked because they have chosen to marry. This, in spite of the fact that history clearly shows that there were even popes who had children, some with multiple partners. This deeply entrenched Catholic belief is predicated on the false assumption that the Pope is the 'vicar' of Christ and the successor of the Apostle Peter. The fallacy continues by saying that Peter was not married. The bible teaches clearly that Peter was not the head of the church[96] and that he was married.[97] Those statements the bible says are doctrines of devils and the preceding scriptures contradict this foundation of Catholicism. By maintaining this misinterpretation of scripture the Catholic Church is attempting to bridle an innate human desire that should be properly expressed in traditional marriage. The evidence has shown that in this regard, the "church" has failed miserably and will continue to do so. The bible is clear,

---

[94]   Gen. 9:3

[95]   1 Cor. 8:8- 13

[96]   Acts 15:13-21, Gal. 2:9

[97]   Matt 8:14, 1 Cor. 9:5

the teaching and propagation of this doctrine of not permitting marriage is taught by demons.

Human Rights

Reeling from the oppression and devastation of WW2, the nations of the world wanted to articulate a set of fundamental 'rights' to which all human beings were entitled. This resulted in the Universal Declaration of Human Rights drafted by the United Nations in 1948. Over the years, the thirty articles contained therein have found their way into various constitutions and international treaties around the world.

The civil rights movement in the United States in the 1950's and 1960's harnessed the frustrations caused by the social and economic oppression of Black Americans (African Americans) and resulted in privileges being given to that racial minority group. Capitalizing on the success of the civil rights movement, each successive decade has seen at least one group or another lobbying for its 'rights' from the 'oppressive' systems around it. This privilege was soon extended to individuals demanding what they perceived as their 'right' to bodily autonomy. The case of Roe v Wade is a classic example of what we are discussing. The so called oppression of women by men, led to the rise of the 'feminist' movement and subsequent gender role confusion. Many women forayed into realms previously dominated by men to prove that they were just as capable. In the process though, many lost the femininity that made them unique as women and most importantly, mothers, and society is reaping a whirlwind as evidenced by the confused children that are the collateral damage of this ideology!

We have progressively moved toward elevating the rights of the individual above the rights and freedoms of the greater community, thereby making the majority captive to the pronouncements of a minority! The problem with this approach is that there is certain selfishness at the heart of individual rights as evidenced by the loss of another's personal right for each 'individual right' gained. So, a woman may have been given the legal right to abort her unborn child, but the unborn child's right to life is trampled on in order to give the woman that privilege. We have seen organizations allowing men to compete in women's competitions and no thought is given to the 'rights' of the majority so that an 'individual right' can be advanced. In other words, as a society we have allowed a minority of individuals to have 'rights' that disproportionately and adversely affect the majority of other individuals and the larger community in the name of 'equity'. This is devilish and is reminiscent of satan introducing the concept of 'self above all else', when he contrived a plan to dispossess God of His ascendant position as God. We allow a minority of humans to trample on a majority of other humans in order to advance their special brand of 'rights' and we do it at the expense of age old tried and true community stabilizing values and simple common sense.

While this has been discussed briefly in the previous chapter, I thought it prudent to say just a few more words. Concerning those who call themselves transgender, I must emphasize that according to the Bible, no such creation exists. It is equally true that based on objective science, no such thing exists either; one either has a 'Y' chromosome, found in males, or they do not! The Bible is clear that God made two distinct physical representations of the sexes, male and female.[98] God does not create confusion[99], so *He* could not have put incompatible spirits in a body; but that does not negate that fact that a person could choose to allow entrance to a contrary spirit! This confusion about the very essence of who a person is must be demonically inspired. The person who claims to be transgender has been lied to about who they are and they believe it. Initially, they may have been tormented by demons in order to get them to agree with the lie. The torment usually subsides when they accept the lie and are embraced in a community of the similarly deceived.

Remember that a person can never rise above the lie he or she believes.

It is upon accepting the contrary thoughts and feelings, that the person either accepts the contrary spirit making them a transgender person or a demon as a dominant spirit and they are now used to advertise this lifestyle option to those who may be presented with similar feelings. The effect is obviously multiplied when high profile individuals are the spokespersons for this 'lifestyle'. In a society open to these ideas, this allows widespread propagation, acceptance and entrenchment of the abnormal and perverse.

---

[98] Matt 19:4

[99] 1 Cor. 14:33

CHAPTER TEN

Freedom

There is a way that seems right to a man, but its end is the way of death (Pro. 16:25)

I am the way, the truth and the life. No one comes to the Father but by Me (John 14:6).

It is for freedom Christ has come to set us free (Gal. 5:1)

The devil is like a roaring lion seeking whom he will devour. Him resist standing steadfast in the faith (1 Pet. 5:8 KJV)

There is only one spirit that was ever intended to control, influence or inspire man and that is the spirit of Almighty God. Man was never to be governed by external laws, but was to have his heart and mind regulated by God Himself. Man of course, could choose to cooperate with God or not. After Adam chose not to obey, all of his offspring thereafter were born outside of the Kingdom of

God and under the authority of an oppressive, controlling spirit that hated God. Jesus Christ came to remedy that problem and offered Himself as the only sacrifice that could pay our sin debt. We must believe that He did this for us and if we do, we become 'born again', spiritually reconnected with the God who made us and desires to have a relationship with us.

The first step to freedom from spiritual darkness and oppression then is to be born again.

We no longer need to experiment with different philosophies in an effort to be right with God. Jesus' sacrifice **alone** *makes us right* with God. God has already done all of the work, He simply asks us to believe it. In other words, once we express faith in Jesus' death and resurrection, God credits Jesus' right standing with Him to us. We become right with God vicariously. We no longer exist in the former 'state of sin', but are now citizens of the Kingdom of God.[100] We will still do and think wrong things as we learn and grow in our relationship with God, but as far as God is concerned, we *ourselves* are right with Him, in our *spirits*. Our challenge is to *learn* how to do what He has asked us to and we will gradually become more like Him in our habits, attitudes and outlook.

The second step is to understand the role of faith. Faith is having confidence in and understanding what God has said about a particular situation and believing it in spite of how things may appear. Know that the enemy's first point of contact with you is through your mind or emotions. Recognize that having impure, angry or self deprecating thoughts, feelings and desires suddenly

---

[100] Col 1:13

come upon you is *not* sin, but an attack from the enemy that must be resisted. The strength needed to resist wave after wave of demonic attacks can be enormous, but it can only be maintained by faith. You must remember that Christ came to set you free from whatever might be a habit, addiction or proclivity. There is the process of learning to develop inner confidence, despite shortcomings and failings, that God has already freed you from your sin or bondage, no matter what you may have done. You must remember as noted above, that Colossians 1:13 teaches that you *have been* rescued from being *dominated* or *controlled* by the power or influences of darkness and that you have been placed into the kingdom of His Son.

We reiterate again that God is not *planning* on setting you free from the power of sin, *He already has.* Unfortunately, you still have memories and emotions of past events that can cause feelings of condemnation, but when you accept the fact of your freedom as truth, confess and act on it contrary to your thoughts and feelings, it will eventually become your lived reality. Freedom is maintained with effort. This is why we are urged to be vigilant.[101]

God has already delivered us from the devils grip (controlling influence), but we must believe it when faced with the stimulus response cycle. So, you must recognize that even though a thought or feeling is telling you that you are still under its control, the Lord says you are free and you must choose to believe Him. As you continue to believe and act accordingly, the intensity of the thoughts, feelings and desires will diminish.

---

[101]   1 Pet. 5:8

Thirdly, knowing who you are based on what God says about you will make it much easier to reject thoughts and urges that try to tell you that you are something else. This is especially true if a person's mind and emotions were adversely altered from sinful experiences. They will have a false self image that has to be corrected. It is from this position that you can better identify ideas, urges and impulses that come from unclean spirits and then choose to reject them. Consistent repetitive rejection of demonic urges coupled with right actions result in the person regaining self control and freedom in that particular area of their lives. Freedom therefore is generally not a onetime experience, but a journey.

Know that if you yield to the temptation you have given the inciting spirit legal ground to operate in you and possibly to bring in other spirits. The more you yield to temptation, the greater the controlling influence the unclean spirit will have and the greater the likelihood that additional spirits will enter to take up residence as well. However, you must also know that based on 1 John 1:9-10, if you confess your sins, the legal right the enemy has is taken away and that spirit is made to leave your spirit. Understand that as a believer in Jesus Christ, simple confession of your sin prompts God Himself not only to forgive you but to cleanse your spirit from the presence of the enemy. You must appreciate though that they may still remain around you to look for opportunities to regain access. Remember, when you sin, confess it, believe He has forgiven you and keep going forward.

We are reminded of the man in Luke 11:21-22 who guarded and safeguarded himself from the enemy's attacks, and we are encouraged to remember that as long as we are in the body, we are at war with the enemy of God. That is why we are challenged to be right thinking and always on our guard, because our adversary the devil walks about like a roaring lion seeking whom he may devour; he is resisted by standing strong in the faith.[102]

This brings us to the last point, we cannot think rightly if we do not know what God says about how we are to live our lives. Remember disobedience to God's word creates an opportunity for the enemy to gain access to the believer. We must learn what he wants us to do and make every effort to do it. It is only when one tries to obey the bible that we can begin to see how brainwashed we have been by our culture.

It is imperative to remember that one of the reasons that God sacrificed His Son was so that we can be free from the *power* of sin. We must keep our focus on this truth. His blood has paid the price so that sin can no longer have a grip on us. We may live under the law of gravity, but we have learned how to walk uprightly, falling less and less with time!

For those who have faith in Christ, you are already legally free through the atoning work of Christ, now the mind must be transformed to accept, believe and act on the truth. The influences in the world will always encourage us to reject God's ways and wisdom. Feelings of condemnation and inadequacy may always arise. We cannot stand against the deluge of sensory and visual stimulation trying to shape our way of thinking if we do not limit our access to it and learn how God desires us to live. We must choose to incorporate His mind and desires into our lives,

---

[102]   1 Pet. 5:8

understanding that people without our perspective will ridicule our efforts.

Read the bible, obey Jesus' commands, nurture a personal relationship with Him and all will be well. It may not be easy, but it will be well! God has made provision for anyone to break free from *any* sin, bondage or controlling spirit through the sacrifice of His son!

CHAPTER ELEVEN

The Last Days

Know this first of all, that in the last days mockers will come with their mocking, following after their own lusts, and saying, "Where is the promise of His coming? For ever since the fathers fell asleep, all continues just as it was from the beginning of creation." 2 Pet. 3:3 NASB

It should be relatively clear now, based on our discussion thus far, that the bible teaches there are unseen forces; influences with agendas that use men to carry them out. Thus far we have mainly highlighted dark, evil and malignant forces, simply because they are the most prevalent and pervasive in the world. It is equally important to understand that while the devil has been working behind the scenes to advance his agenda, God has not been asleep. One way that He has consistently tried to give mankind hope throughout the millennia is through prophecy. God alone is able to given authoritative declarations about what is going to happen and no one can stop it.[103]

The second thing that prophecy does is that it allows us to see that the bible can be trusted. Written by multiple authors over thousands of years it has a consistent theme, the sovereignty of God. The ultimate triumph of His purposes over all others! Biblical prophecy is different from the writings of prognosticators like Nostradamus, Edgar Cayce and others simply because in 100% of instances bible prophecy will be fulfilled. No other fortune teller or others with similar abilities could boast of even approaching a 100% accuracy rate.

For the sake of simplicity this brief discussion on prophecy will be divided into three areas. We can consider, for brevity's sake, prophecies about the coming of the Messiah and the kingdom of God, secondly, prophecies about Israel and her existence and finally prophecies about the future.

It is fairly easy to find information regarding fulfilled bible prophecy; I find that it is prophecy of future events that causes people to have the most doubt. It is important to remember though, that when prophecies were made in the past, their fulfillment looked to the future and generations not seeing their fulfillment could easily question the veracity of the prophecies. We must also remember that just as surely as past events were in the future of those hearing these prophecies for the first time, soon too, prophecies made in the past will be in the future. We will consider just a few prophecies, firstly, concerning Jesus:

---

[103] Isa. 46:10

- The very first prophecy in scripture was given in Genesis 3:15 immediately after the fall of man. God made a pronouncement, that an offspring of the woman would one day crush the head of the devil.

- 700 years before Jesus was born Isaiah 7:14, recorded that a **virgin** would have a son and his name would mean God with us. He further said that the Messiah would establish a kingdom on the earth and He will have a kingdom which will not end.[104]

- Approximately 700 BC the prophet Micah said the Messiah would be born in Bethlehem.[105]

- Daniel wrote approximately 550 BC that from the time of the Babylonian empire three additional kingdoms would come to the world scene. It is believed and history supports that those additional kingdoms were the Medo-Persians, Greeks and Romans. It says in Daniel 2:44 that in the times of the fourth kingdom God would set up a kingdom that will never be destroyed. It was during the times of the Roman kingdom that Jesus started preaching the gospel of the kingdom of God. Daniel also states that the Kingdom of God will grow until it fills the whole earth.

There are additional references that state that the Messiah would be sold for the price of a slave, thirty pieces of silver, (Zech. 11:12-13), crucified, not one of his bones would be broken and

---

104   Isa. 9: 6-8
105   Micah 5:2

people would verbally abuse him and divide his clothes among themselves (Psalm 22). In addition, Jesus himself said that He would rise again from the dead. In spite of these passages, there are still those who question the veracity and authenticity of the bible.

Let us also consider that there are multiple prophecies concerning the nation of Israel:

- That they would go into the land of Egypt and remain there for 400 years as slaves and then would be delivered and would come out with great possessions (Gen. 15: 12-14).
- Would settle in the land of Canaan (Gen. 15:18, 17:8).
- Would sin against God and be driven from their land and carried away as captives Deut. 28: 49-52, Dan. 9:24-26) and would return for a season (Jer. 32:36-37)
- The temple would be destroyed (2 Chron. 7:19-22, Matt. 24:1-2).
- In the last days the people of Israel would return to the land (Eze. 34:13) and will never be completely destroyed (Lev. 26:44).

Please consider that if such specific prophecies were made thousands of years ago and if future prophecies have been made which will come to pass, shouldn't we at least entertain the other truths the bible teaches? The truth about the devil and his workings, the way spirits use and discard men for their *own* purposes and the advancement of a global anti-God agenda.

Now concerning the future, the bible states explicitly that there will be an increase in wickedness, wars and ethnic (race against race) uprisings. Just look around! We must also remember that in Acts 2:17, God has promised to pour out His spirit upon all flesh in the last days as well. The gospel of the kingdom will be preached to the entire world and *then* the end would come. After that would be the judgment.

References to all of the above events can be found in Matt: 24, more specific details are found in the book of Revelation and other books.

The bible also teaches in 2 Timothy 3: 1-6, that in the last days terrible times will come, people will disregard God and His word, will be cold, unforgiving, lovers of money and without self control, they will ridicule God's word and follow after their own desires. [106] There is no denying that all that has been said describes the prevalent cultures of this world today. We have already discussed how all of these conditions are not only evidences of evil spirits exerting control over men, but also displays their disregard for the things of God as well.

Various churches have capitulated to the social pressures that evil is presenting in these days, and those who have not joined the enemy are completely silent on issues relating to the transgender community, same sex unions and other 'sensitive' topics for fear of being viewed as hateful or discriminatory. We often forget that this world and its systems are impermanent and will ultimately be judged by God. The silence and compromise of the church emboldens the enemy, so that perversion is finding more creative

---

[106]   2Pet. 3:3

outlets to desensitize the remainder of the population that disagree with the cornucopia of ungodly ideologies in our midst.

In fact it is now abundantly clear that the focus of their efforts is on children. For, if certain inclinations can be planted in the hearts and minds of children at a very early age, it will be quite difficult for them to overcome that tilt without God's help. It is difficult to turn on the television without seeing a commercial or a program that is not offensive or geared towards desensitizing children to the perverse. The response to this surge of evil is not being adequately opposed by believers.

Political correctness is a tool of the devil.

There are those who say that Jesus promised that He would return, but it has already been 2000 years. They scoff at the idea that He will come again and use the seeming non-fulfillment of this prophecy to argue against the existence of God or the veracity of the bible. As stated before, a close reading of Matt 24:14 says that the gospel of the kingdom will be preached in the whole world… and **then** the end will come. For the past 2000 years the gospel of the kingdom has not been preached significantly. For the most part the religion of Christianity has been promoted; various denominational doctrines of faith, repentance, grace and other creeds have been taught and propagated, but not the Kingdom of God. Only in the past few decades have there been more accessible teachings and more understanding about that Kingdom.

People need to know that God is the sovereign ruler of all and our Father. We were spiritually separated from Him by sin, evidenced by our birth into a world opposed to Him. He made a way for us to be reconnected to Him so that we could become sons again, who exercise the dominion He has given us in this realm. We have an opportunity to get to know Him personally and have Him regulate our hearts and minds from *within*. For, the kingdom of God is *in* those who believe in Him.[107] This allows His kingdoms influence to manifest in the earth realm and enables others to be released from the darkness of this worlds systems and to also become His sons, members of His family and partakers of all that is His for all eternity. God is not mans enemy, the devil is!

It is hoped that this short study has shared some light on that Kingdom, that the readers would have gained some insight into workings of the unseen world and some understanding of how to better navigate it and overcome during our brief time in this reality.

---

[107] Luke 17:21 KJV

SPIRITUAL LAWS

The following are *some* of the spiritual laws outlined in this book:

- God creates by faith.
- Man, who is made in the image of God also creates by faith. Whatever a man can 'see' in the unseen recesses of his mind (imagine), he can create.
- It is mans ability to create that makes him useful to God or the devil, in the earth.
- Earth is the domain of man, not God. Man is responsible for what manifests in it.
- Man was made to be regulated within by Gods spirit. After the fall, any spirit a man yields to is the spirit that will control him.
- God can only relate spirit to spirit.
- The sole purpose of the body is to manifest the unseen in the physical realm.
- When a person loses control of self, other spirits can enter that person's body and function in the earth realm.

- Spirits may be transferred from one person to another person or to objects.
- Deceased human spirits can continue to exist in another person's body.
- Thought, desire and action cause a man to become a thing, anything.
- A man becomes what he thinks on and believes.
- You cannot rise above the lies you believe.
- The truth is the only antidote to a lie.
- A person does not get to choose/control what kind of spirit enters them.
- Being born again reconnects a person to God spirit to spirit.
- Sustained faith in Christ's victory over sin and the devil for the believer will give him victory over any sin.
- A born again believer has power and authority over unclean spirits.

Also by the Author:

Insights into CREATION, the Nephilim *and the* Sons of GOD

IAN ARCHER

www.insightsfromthebible.com

Printed in the United States
by Baker & Taylor Publisher Services